L

W
De
LO
N

This
by

OXFORD MEDICAL PUBLICATIONS

Cancer

THE FACTS

Cancer

THE FACTS

BY
RONALD BODLEY SCOTT

OXFORD
OXFORD UNIVERSITY PRESS
NEW YORK TORONTO
1979

Oxford University Press, Walton Street, Oxford OX2 6DP

OXFORD LONDON GLASGOW
NEW YORK TORONTO MELBOURNE WELLINGTON
IBADAN NAIROBI DAR ES SALAAM LUSAKA CAPE TOWN
KUALA LUMPUR SINGAPORE JAKARTA HONG KONG TOKYO
DELHI BOMBAY CALCUTTA MADRAS KARACHI

British Library Cataloguing in Publication Data

Scott, *Sir* Ronald Bodley
    Cancer. – (Oxford medical publications).
    1. Cancer
    I. Title   II. Series
    616.9'94   RC261   79-40483
    ISBN 0-19-261149-6

Typeset by Hope Services Ltd., Abingdon
Printed in Great Britain
by R. Clay & Co. Ltd., Bungay

TO
G.H.F.

Preface

There are few people who have not had a friend or relative who has suffered from cancer. Indeed one-fifth of all deaths in England and Wales are due to this disease. Nevertheless ignorance of the subject is profound and from this ignorance springs the unnecessary and ill-founded dread which the very word 'cancer' inspires. This book is written with the aim of providing those without medical knowledge with an account of the more important facts about cancer. Only knowledge and understanding will dispel the myths and superstitions which surround the subject. Most people nowadays believe they should be informed about illness, should be able to understand the reasons for the treatment recommended, and should be aware of the likely outcome. No-one can deny a man these rights when he himself is the patient, if only because treatment requires his full and intelligent co-operation.

This book is divided into two parts. In the first the general problems of cancer are discussed and in the second there is a more detailed consideration of the many different varieties of the disease. In the first section attention is given to the recognized provoking causes of cancer, the frequency of the disease, the tests required for diagnosis, the forms of treatment available, and the outlook. The purely medical details which concern the doctor but not the patient or potential patient are omitted. Much, it must be confessed, makes depressing reading. The title of the book, *Cancer: The Facts*, requires the facts be recorded and no good purpose is served by concealing the truth. On the other hand, there is much which is encouraging and the immense advances of the past 25 years give every reason for an optimistic view of the future.

I make no apology for this objective account of malignant

Preface

disease. Many years of practice have convinced me that the sick prefer to know the facts. They are seldom deceived by the hollow charade which some feel obligatory and are often bitterly resentful when they suspect that the truth is being hidden from them.

It is a pleasure to record my gratitude to my friends Mr Donald McGavin MChir FRCS and Professor Michael Whitehouse for their kindness in reading my manuscript and for their helpful suggestions.

I am indebted to my former colleagues at St. Bartholemew's Hospital, Dr Alfred Stansfeld, Dr Gordon Canti, Dr Janet Dacie, and Dr Adrian Dixon for the illustrations.

R.B.S.
January 1979

Contents

1

The nature of cancer

The word 'cancer' is familiar to everyone, but there are few who would be capable of an accurate definition. Popular imagination sees it as a disease which is always incurable and which advances ineluctably until, after a course of unremitting and increasing pain, it ends in death. Its cause is held to be unknown. Some still believe it may be a retribution for past sins. Only one of these beliefs has any basis in fact: it is true that the ultimate cause is unknown. It is no matter for surprise that these sinister myths and deep-rooted superstitions have endowed cancer with such an emotional charge that merely to pronounce the word is taboo. Such unreasoning dread can only be exorcized by knowledge and understanding. This book is written with the aim and the hope of providing those without a medical training with a clearer understanding of this common disease.

In order to communicate their thoughts to their colleagues all scientists devise jargon peculiar to themselves and incomprehensible to the uninitiated. Doctors, some of whom claim the title of 'medical scientist', have their own professional language and become so accustomed to its use that they often find difficulty in explaining the problems of illness in terms which can be understood by their patients, and for this reason definitions are necessary. It is logical to start with an attempt to explain what is meant by the word 'cancer' itself. In Latin 'cancer' means a crab and with the earlier form 'canker' it has been used since 1600 in much the same sense as it is now. Then it described a creeping ulcer which gradually spread, eating away and destroying the tissues in its neighbourhood. During the past century the taboo attached to the word has led to a number of circumlocutions designed to avoid its use. A common one is 'new growth' or its Greek

1

Cancer — the facts

equivalent, 'neoplasm'; another is 'tumour' which literally means no more than a swelling—cancer often makes its appearance as an abnormal swelling. In a different category is 'carcinoma'. This word, although derived from καρκινος, the Greek for crab, is now restricted to certain types of cancer arising from the covering tissues, the skin, and mucous membranes, and from the glands. Another word, 'sarcoma' is used to describe cancer arising from the body's supporting structures — bones, muscle, tendons, and fibrous tissue.

Cancer is a disorder of cellular behaviour. Everyone is familiar with the story of the body's development from one single cell formed by the union of the male sperm and the female egg. This cell divides into two and these two divide again. Division of their progeny continues generation after generation and the cells thus formed undergo progressive alterations to fit them for the various roles they are destined to play when growth is complete. The cell is thus the body's basic unit and even when it is fully grown, cells continue to divide, replacing worn out tissue, repairing injuries, and healing wounds. Such complex, but orderly, processes of growth, development, and repair clearly require some integrating central control. An analogy has been drawn between the body and the nation. The second consists of individuals each retaining the capacity for voluntary action, but local authority and, superior to it, central government control and direct their actions to ensure that they do not run counter to the interests of the state. The body is likewise composed of individual cells which preserve some degree of autonomy. Each contains a mechanism — believed to reside in the genes — which controls its behaviour. Nevertheless there are overriding external influences which in health make sure that the activities of every cell conform to the needs of the body as a whole.

It is a disturbance of this controlling mechanism, leading to disorder of cell growth, which underlies cancer. The defect lies within the cell itself. This is proved by the observation that cancer cells transplanted from an animal with a cancer

The nature of cancer

to another of the same species will continue to divide in the recipient and give rise to a cancer indistinguishable from that of the donor animal. The cells of all cancers are marked by a disorder of growth due to some fault within the cell itself. Once established in a cell this fault is heritable and transmitted to all succeeding generations of that cell. Nevertheless it is impossible to define it more exactly than to say that the disorder is one of uncontrolled and purposeless growth — indeed, no single other feature has been identified as common to all cancer cells and it is possible that none exists.

Cancers behave in a fashion described as malignant and the term 'malignant' disease is often used as a synonym. This adjective contributes to the general air of hopelessness by its unfounded implication that the disease is always incurable, but it is also used in a more technical sense to describe certain features by which cancers can be recognized when examined by the pathologist. These are discussed in Chapter 3.

The definition given above does no more than describe in general terms the basic change in the cancerous process — the sudden appearance of grossly disordered behaviour which the affected cell or cells transmit to all cells derived from them. Thus the word 'cancer' comes to be used in two quite different senses: first, as a description of the ill-understood cellular change noted in earlier paragraphs and common to all malignant growths and, secondly, as the pattern of illness this cancerous change causes. This second depends upon the organ or tissue which is the seat of the malignant tumour and explains the remark, often made, that cancer is not a single disease but a group of diseases. It is not necessary to labour the point that a cancer which arises in the lung will cause a different kind of illness from one which arises in the stomach, even though the fundamental disturbance in the cells of the two organs is the same. A second variable is in the rate at which the cancer cells divide, for this determines the rate at which the cancer grows. In different organs and at different ages this differs widely, in youth often being rapid and middle age slow. Consequently the aggressive qualities of malignant tumours vary from patient to patient even when they arise in the same organ.

A final variable lies in the soil in which the cancer grows — the patient himself. It is difficult to measure the influence which the individual and his tissues exert upon the disease which affects him. It is certain that he is not a passive vehicle. At another level it is unreasonable to suppose that all the imponderables which make up a man's 'constitution' are without influence. Even more difficult to assess is the effect of the patient's attitude to his illness. Some reject the very notion that they have cancer; others, accepting the doctor's verdict, will face the disease with an aggressive resistance to its inroads; and yet others will display no more than passive resignation. No doctor of experience would be prepared to discount the importance of these factors.

2

The causes of cancer

The basic nature of the cancerous process has been described in the last chapter. It is a disorder of cellular growth in which the cells are no longer subject to the restraining influences normally controlling their behaviour. The fault causing this disorder is generally held to reside in the genes—the factors within the cell which determine character and inheritance. Once established this fault is irreversible and transmitted to succeeding generations of the cells in which it first developed. Many hypotheses have been suggested to account for the postulated genetic change and indeed some research workers are not prepared to accept the fundamental cause as being of this order. The various explanations offered need only brief description.

In animals many cancers are known to be due to infection by viruses. A virus is so small that it cannot be seen with the ordinary microscope. It is incapable of independent life and develops within the cells of the man or animal it invades, becoming incorporated in and subverting the genetic apparatus. Virus may pass from parent to offspring and this might explain some hereditary cancers. It is tempting to try and account for human cancer by this mechanism. In only one variety is there even suggestive evidence of such a connection. The Burkitt tumour is a common cancer of Africans in whom it is almost constantly associated with the presence of a virus known as the Epstein–Barr or EB virus. Nevertheless the part the virus plays, if any, in the cause of the cancer is unknown. Ultimate proof that a human cancer had a viral cause could only be provided by the obviously indefensible experiment of showing that it developed in a human subject after inoculation with the virus.

A view which held the field for many years and remains

implicit in many of the other hypotheses is that of 'somatic mutation'. This assumes that the genes are not always reproduced in an orderly normal manner, but that from time to time one develops a fault with the power to disorganize cell growth. If this abnormal gene survives, the fault is transmitted to its descendants and their continued division will give rise to a cancer. This genetic abnormality, it is suggested, could be brought about either by chance or by the action of any number of external agencies. These external factors, which may act as what are known as 'carcinogens', are discussed later in this chapter.

What might be called the reverse of this explanation regards the cell as provided with various restraining or controlling mechanisms. When these operate normally orderly development and cellular behaviour result. If one or more of them are 'lost' in the process of development, cell growth is no longer subject to restraint and becomes disorganized and uncontrolled.

During recent years another theory has gained popularity because it seems to have application to all forms of cancer and offers a unifying explanation. This assumes that a gene capable of causing cancerous growth is normally present in all human cells, but that it remains inactive or 'repressed'. It is known that a number of genes normally present are in this inoperative state. For various reasons the repression may be lifted, the gene becomes 'derepressed' and active leading to the unrestrained cell growth we know as cancer.

None of these hypotheses is completely satisfying because the spectrum of cancer is so wide that exceptions which cannot be explained are easy to find. A number of factors are known which appear to play parts of greater or lesser importance in its cause although how they operate is seldom clear. Some may induce the postulated genetic changes; in others the mechanism is quite unknown. They are discussed in the following paragraphs.

The causes of cancer

Heredity

It is hard to establish the importance of heredity as a cause of human cancer because man is of such mixed ancestry. Members of the same family moreover share the same environment often making it difficult to distinguish between causes which are hereditary and those which are environmental. In animals where pure breeds can be developed and the environment controlled, cancers, proven to be hereditary, are common.

In man, the commonest is the retinoblastoma, a malignant growth which develops in the retina of the eye in infants and young children. It occurs in about one live birth in 20 000 and in 5–10 per cent other members of the family are affected.

A number of hereditary diseases are spoken of as 'pre-cancerous'. In these, although the condition is benign, there is a greatly increased risk, sometimes amounting to certainty, of it later becoming malignant. An example is familial polyposis of the colon in which members of a family are prone to develop numerous fleshy wart-like growths (polyps) in the large bowel. These are initially benign, but with the passage of time inevitably develop cancerous change.

Many studies of families have been made. Clear-cut instances of hereditary influence are excessively rare, but there is a suggestion that certain families have an increased susceptibility to cancer, although seldom to cancer of any specific organ. This increase is seldom more than that expected in the general population.

Race

The influence of race is difficult to disentangle from that of environment. Nevertheless there are examples of clear racial predisposition to some specific type of cancer. The most striking of these is the relative frequency of cancer of the nasopharynx – the area at the back of the nose – in Southern Chinese. The reverse of the coin is the rarity of cancer of the breast in Japanese women. Both these anomalies of incidence persist in Chinese or Japanese who have emigrated from their homelands.

7

Cancer – the facts

Viral infection

The possibility of cancer having a viral cause has been discussed in earlier paragraphs. It remains to consider whether viral infection may be an occasional factor rather than the universal cause. The association of the Epstein–Barr virus with the Burkitt tumour has been mentioned and there is evidence of its frequent presence in the nasopharyngeal cancer of the Southern Chinese. Viruses are, however, universally and constantly present and can frequently be recovered from cancers. This does not establish them as the cause. The cancer cells may offer a favourable soil for development of the virus and it may be 'a passenger and not the driver'.

Chemical agents

The first indication that exposure to chemical agents might cause cancer dates back to 1775. Percival Pott, Surgeon to St. Bartholomew's Hospital, noted that chimney sweeps begrimed with soot were peculiarly liable to cancer of the scrotum. A century later cancer of the urinary bladder was found to be unduly common in workers in the dye industry. Over the following years it came to be recognized that certain occupations carried a high risk of malignant disease. These included cancer of the lung in workers in chromium, nickel, and asbestos; cancer of the bladder in those employed in the rubber industry; cancer of the nasal sinuses in some woodworkers in the furniture trade; and recently an otherwise rare form of cancer of the liver in makers of the plastic, polyvinyl chloride.

The appreciation of these industrial hazards suggested that exposure to chemical substances unrelated to occupation might be an important cause of cancer. It stimulated much experimental research to determine which chemical agents carried this danger and to devise methods of assessing the risk of exposure to them. A connection has been firmly established only in two: the first in cancer of the lung and cigarette smoking, and the second cancer of the mouth and

The causes of cancer

tongue and the chewing of betel nut or tabacco. So much has been written on the first that repetition would be tedious. It is sufficient to say that the risk of cancer of the lung is in direct proportion to the number of cigarettes smoked and that deaths from this cause are twenty times more numerous in heavy smokers than in non-smokers. In a different category is the rare cancer of the vagina which may appear in teenage girls whose mothers have taken a man-made drug with hormone-like effects—diethylstilboestrol—in the first half of pregnancy to prevent miscarriage.

A number of naturally occurring substances have recently come under suspicion of being carcinogenic. One of importance is aflatoxin, the product of a mould which may contaminate unhygienically stored meal. It is a powerful carcinogen in animals and is suspected of being responsible for the frequency of cancer of the liver in Asians and Africans. Cyclamate, a synthetic sweetening agent, given in high doses for long periods in rats, may lead to cancer of the bladder. It has been withdrawn from sale in this country and the United States.

It has been recognized for years that cancer of the large bowel is commoner in those who live in Western countries than in the natives of Asia and Africa. It was suggested that a carcinogenic agent, related to Western diet and habits, might be operative in the bowel. Such a diet is known to favour the growth of certain bacteria capable of converting the bile normally present in the bowel into identifiable carcinogens. The diet of African and Asian natives contains much vegetable fibre leaving bulky residues which pass rapidly through the bowel. In the Western world, constipation is common and the slow transit of the bowel contents ensures prolonged exposure to the postulated carcinogen.

Thus the number of human cancers proved to be due to chemical agents, artificially occurring or man-made, is small. There are however several in which such a cause is suspected and growing belief that the great majority of common cancers will eventually prove to originate in this way. It is this that

9

has stimulated research into chemical agents as a cause of cancer in animals.

The first to point the way were Yamagiwa and Ichikawa in 1916 when they showed that repeated painting of the ear of a rabbit with tar resulted in cancer of the skin. Since then many substances have been found to be carcinogenic for animals. It is uncertain how often a chemical substance capable of causing cancer in animals is likely to be similarly dangerous to man. However it is probably relevant that every agent known to be carcinogenic in man has proved capable of causing cancer in animals. Tests have been devised for the routine testing of drugs in the hopes of excluding this danger and only when their safety has been established beyond reasonable doubt are they licensed for sale. In animal tests the substances are commonly administered in strengths many times greater and over periods far longer than would apply in man.

Radiation

There are several well-attested examples of radioactivity or ionizing radiation causing cancer in man, but it is far more difficult to provide proof of its wider importance. Its dangers first became apparent when the pioneers of radiology began to develop cancer of the skin exposed to X-rays. The first case was reported only a few years after Roentgen's discovery. In 1911 it was suggested that leukaemia might result from such exposure, but the truth of this contention was only established beyond question after the detonation of the atomic bomb in Japan. Not only was there an increase in the incidence of leukaemia in those who survived the initial explosion, but this increase was greater the nearer the survivor had been to its epicentre. In Hiroshima leukaemia in survivors within 1000 metres of the epicentre was 60 times more common than in the general population of Japan. Support comes from the finding that in men receiving X-ray treatment for ankylosing spondylitis, a form of arthritis in the spine, the frequency of leukaemia was 9.5 times that of men with this disease who were not treated in this way. It should be noted that when it was prescribed, radiotherapy was the accepted treatment for this disease and the risk was unsuspected. In both these men and in the Japanese it was a particular variety of leukaemia, the myeloid or granulocytic type, which developed.

Ionizing radiation may lead to cancer of bone (osteosarcoma). This was proved many years ago in workers painting figures in luminous paint on the dials of clocks and watches. The paint contained radium or mesothorium and the dangerous properties of neither were known at that time. The workers were accustomed to point their brushes between their lips before applying the paint. The radioactive material was absorbed and depositing in the bones where after 10–25 years cancer developed.

Irradiation of the neck in infants and young children has been followed by cancer of the thyroid gland; the incidence of this tumour rose in infants of the Marshall Islands who were exposed to nuclear fall-out and in survivors of the atomic bomb explosions in Japan. The frequency of cancer of the lung in the pitch-blende miners of Saxony and Bohemia first noted in the sixteenth century and in the uranium miners in the United States is almost certainly due to the radioactivity of the ores.

Immunity

In diseases due to infection the body is able to recognize the microbes responsible as 'foreign' and to form protective substances, called antibodies, which will attack the invaders. Some laboratory tests suggest that cancer cells are identified as 'foreign' and may provoke a similar reaction. Whether this mechanism plays any protective role in human cancer is doubtful. Nevertheless it has been noted that when the apparatus which forms antibodies is incompetent or its activity suppressed by drugs, cancers are more liable to arise.

11

Cancer – the facts

Injury and inflammation

There is little scientific evidence that physical injury can result in malignant disease. Popular superstition allots it a role in the cause of cancer of the breast, but there is no support for this myth. It is true that plaintiffs have often been awarded damages on a plea that they have developed cancer after an injury, but a decision in the courts does not rank as scientific evidence.

Cancer does at times develop at the site of long-continued inflammation. Before antibiotics controlled infection chronic abscesses with persistent discharge were common and might remain unhealed for 30 years or more. Sometimes a cancer would form at the mouth of the track through which this discharge reached the skin. In patients with ulcerative colitis, in which there is extensive chronic ulceration of the mucous lining of the large bowel, the risk of cancerous change in the colon is high. It increases with the duration of the disease and with its extent in the bowel; after 20 years it is probably above 25 per cent.

Cancer may arise too in the scar left by a burn. It was once frequent for Indian peasants to keep warm by carrying an earthenware vessel containing smouldering charcoal held beneath their clothes by a strap around the waist. It was known as a kangri and the skin upon which it rested became hardened and coarse, finally undergoing malignant change. Cancer of the gullet (oesophagus) may develop in the scar which follows swallowing a corrosive liquid such a lysol— once a common method of attempting suicide.

There is no question that prolonged exposure to intense sunlight increases the liability to skin cancer. This accounts for the frequency with which a cancerous type of mole (malignant melanoma) and other forms of skin cancer affect those of European descent who live in such places as North Queensland.

Parasites

Cancer of the urinary bladder is one of the commonest

The causes of cancer

forms of malignant disease in Egypt. This is the result of infection with a parasite called *Schistosoma haematobium* which over 80 per cent of fellaheen acquire. It is found too in other parts of Africa. The schistosoma invades the wall of the bladder where it gives rise to a chronic inflammation which finally progresses to cancer.

When considering the various factors which may play a part in the cause of cancer it is important to preserve a sense of proportion. With the exceptions of cancer of the lung and smoking, cancer of the mouth and the chewing of betel nut, and cancer of the bladder and schistosomiasis, the cause can seldom be identified or the type of cancer is extremely rare. For instance, in patients with leukaemia the frequency with which a story of exposure to ionizing radiation can be obtained is not above 3 or 4 per cent. Similarly the cancer of the liver which workers in the polyvinyl chloride industry may develop is one of exceptional rarity. In the vast majority of patients the cancer arises spontaneously and none of the causal factors discussed can be inculpated. Their importance lies partly in their providing clues which can be followed in the search for the cause of malignant disease in general and partly in the preventive measures which will follow from their recognition and control.

Geographical influences

During recent years research workers have become interested in the differences in the incidence of cancer in different countries. It is reasonable to suppose that a markedly higher rate in one country might indicate exposure to some carcinogen operative there. However, it is difficult to draw firm conclusions because racial, occupational, cultural, and genetic differences exist between different populations and it is often impossible to decide how much an increase in cancer is due to one or more of these factors and how much to some environmental cause depending upon geography.

Examples of cultural influence have already been mentioned.

13

Cancer – the facts

They include the frequency of cancer of the tongue and mouth in India due to chewing betel nut and tobacco and of cancer of the lung in the United Kingdom and the United States caused by cigarette smoking. The nasopharyngeal cancer of the Southern Chinese and the rarity of cancer of the breast in Japanese women are instances of genetic influence.

Perhaps the main importance of identifying geographical variations is that it can lead to the discovery of carcinogens which could be controlled or eliminated. There are a number of peculiarities of incidence which have yet to be explained but which strongly suggest the notion of a carcinogen operative in a localized geographical region. Cancer of the gullet (oesophagus) is one example. This disease is extremely common in one area of Iran bordering the Caspian Sea. In most countries men are affected more than women: for instance, in Brittany, where it is also common, it is seen ten times more often in men than in women and this preponderance is attributed to smoking and alcohol. In the Iranian province women are affected twice as often as men and almost the whole population is teetotal.

Cancer of the stomach is becoming less common in the United Kingdom and the United States, but its frequency remains unaltered in Japan where it is twenty times that in Mozambique. It is difficult to avoid the conclusion that the Japanese diet must contain a carcinogen. The frequency of primary cancer of the large bowel in the western world compared with that in the Bantu has been discussed. The reverse is true of cancer of the liver: in the Bantu of Mozambique aged 25–34, this disease is 500 times more common than in the white American of the same age. Here again there is reason to suspect a dietary carcinogen.

Another common cancer showing various geographical variations in its frequency is cancer of the cervix or neck of the womb. It is, for instance, twenty-eight times more common in Colombians than in Jewesses born in Israel.

Geography is of predictable importance in determining

the frequency of cancer of the skin. All varieties are more common in the fair-skinned. They occur almost exclusively in the exposed areas of the body and they are far more often seen in regions where there is prolonged sunshine.

These few examples are enough to show how the study of the geographical variations in the incidence of different cancers may throw some light on their cause. The information which has accumulated from reviews of what is called the epidemiology of cancer gives further support to the suggestion that the majority of the common cancers will eventually prove to be due to carcinogenic substances in the environment.

3

The physical forms of cancer

Hitherto cancer has been discussed in terms of cell behaviour, but to the naked eye and to the examining hand it customarily presents itself as a tumour. Literally, this word means no more than a swelling, but in this context it can be defined as an abnormal mass of tissue, the growth of which exceeds and is uncoordinated with that of the normal tissues and which continues to grow in the same way after the cause which initiated the process has vanished. Tumours may be benign or malignant. Benign tumours remain local, they grow slowly and do not threaten life except by reason of their size or by causing pressure on important organs. Malignant tumours are cancers.

The ways in which malignant tumours have been defined have changed with the passage of years and with the advance of knowledge. Cancers were first regarded simply as tumours or swellings which grew causing destruction and ulceration of normal tissues in their vicinity. With the development of the modern microscope some 150 years ago definitions and classifications founded on the appearance revealed by the instrument were devised and it came to be appreciated that the cell was the basic unit, not only of the body as a whole, but of malignant disease. Gradually thoughts turned from the static picture seen down the microscope to contemplation of the disturbances of cell behaviour which led to such pictures. It was finally recognized that the basic difference between the cancer cell and the healthy cell lay in a defective mechanism controlling growth and that this defect was irreversible and transmitted to all the progeny of the malignant cell.

This definition is of necessity phrased in the most general terms. It is not easy to draw a line sharply dividing normal from abnormal growth. When repair is required, for example in the liver, cells may divide at a far greater rate than they do in many cancers, but they cease to do so when the repair has been effected. The difficulty extends also to the appearance of the cancer cell. There are no constant marks which distinguish the cancer cell from the normal cell. It is true that as they divide more rapidly they come to resemble the cells of the embryo, and are thus spoken of as immature; they are seen more often in the process of division than are normal cells. Nevertheless there are no constant characteristics by which they can be identified.

Apart from the individual cells the pattern of their arrangement as seen under the microscope may be almost identical with that in the organ from which the growth springs, but on the other hand it may bear little outward resemblance to it. The situation puts one in mind of Lord Haldane's reply to the Kaiser when asked to define an act of aggression: 'It is hard,' he answered, 'to define a grain of sand, but I can recognize a heap of it when I see one.' Likewise, it is hard to define a malignant cell, but usually easy to recognize a cancer.

The division between benign tumours and malignant or cancerous ones has already been mentioned, but like much else in the study of malignant disease this distinction is not as clear as the two contrasting terms suggest. It is more accurate to think of a spectrum with tumours which are undeniably malignant at one end to those which are equally clearly benign at the other. Between the two extremities are transitional forms which the pathologist may find it difficult to allot to one group or the other. Typically the benign tumour consists of cells which are almost indistinguishable from those of the parent organ and with a similar orderly arrangement. The cells are confined within a membrane or capsule formed by fibrous tissue. The arrangement of blood vessels is likewise orderly and adequate. The tumour grows by expansion and compresses the tissues round about it: it remains localized.

17

Cancer – the facts

The malignant tumour – the cancer – is quite different. It has already been explained that the appearance of the individual cells which make up the tumour and the pattern of their arrangement vary greatly. They may closely resemble those of the parent tissue or they may differ from it so widely that their lineage is impossible to trace. The body reacts to the presence of a growing cancer by developing a scaffolding composed of fibrous tissue which gives the cells support and blood vessels which provide the tumour with nourishment. Frequently the growth of the tumour is so rapid that the scaffolding is inadequate and the blood supply insufficient to meet the demands of the multiplying cells. A proportion then perishes from want of blood. No capsule surrounds the tumour. The microscope shows its cells growing into the normal tissue, spreading into the spaces between the healthy cells and by this process of infiltration invading the neighbouring structures and bringing about their destruction. (see Plates 12 and 13)

The mechanism responsible for invasion is not fully understood. It seems probable that the malignant cells form some substance which damages or actually destroys healthy cells in their neighbourhood, enabling the cancer to thrust its way between them. This may well be helped by the pressure the growing mass of tumour must exert. Cancer cells have some power of spontaneous movement and will break off easily from the main mass of the tumour because they lack the adhesive properties of healthy cells. Sometimes they will burst their way through the thin wall of a vein, become detached and swept along in the current of circulating blood until they come to rest in some distant organ. Here they will anchor, establish themselves, and continue to divide and multiply until they form a colony of the original cancer. Such colonies are spoken of as secondary deposits or metastases to distinguish them from the primary parent tumour. At other times cancer cells will invade a lymphatic vessel and spread along it or travel in the lymph until arrival at lymphatic gland where once again a secondary deposit may form.

The physical forms of cancer

There are therefore three ways in which a cancer spreads. The first is by direct extension as its growing edge penetrates and infiltrates further and further into the healthy tissue in its immediate neighbourhood. The second is by blood-borne fragments of tumour or even single cells being carried by the circulation to form metastases in distant organs. The third, 'lymphatic spread' is by the lymphatic vessels to the lymphatic glands, first to those in the immediate vicinity of the tumour and later to the groups nearest to those first invaded (see Plate 14). A full understanding of this complex process of spread and a precise assessment of the position in the individual patient is essential for the rational planning of retreat.

It is not surprising that the liver and the lungs, organs through which there is a large volume of blood constantly flowing, are the commonest sites for blood-borne secondary deposits. Metastases present many unsolved problems. There are some cancers, particularly those of the breast, thyroid, stomach, prostate, and kidney, which have a peculiar and unexplained liability to give rise to metastases in bones. Sometimes a metastasis declares itself as long as 20 years after the primary tumour has apparently been cured; sometimes what is clearly a metastasis brings the patient to the doctor and no primary tumour can be found.

The second type of metastatic spread is through the lymphatic system. Cancer cells gain entry to the lymph either by way of the blood stream or by the direct penetration of the cancer into a lymphatic channel. They travel to the nearest lymphatic gland and are there arrested. It is likely that if the cells are few in number they are destroyed in the gland. If they overwhelm the protective capacity of the gland they divide and invade its substance to form a metastatic cancer. From such a secondary deposit further spread may occur. Cells may detach themselves and travel by the lymphatic vessels to neighbouring glands. It is believed that pressure on affected glands may sometimes be responsible for this and manipulation during surgical operations is thought to be a potential cause of dissemination of cancer cells. All surgeons are aware of this possible danger and take what steps they can to avoid it.

It is by no means unusual to find enlarged glands in the neighbourhood of a cancer and for these glands when examined to prove free from malignant cells, showing only an overgrowth of normal elements. Many believe that such glands have a protective function and prevent cells from the cancer spreading by the lymphatic channels. The anatomical design of the lymphatic glands suggests that they may act as filters and it is known that many of the cells of which they are composed are capable of forming antibodies.

There has therefore been some controversy over the removal of the neighbouring lymphatic glands at operations for cancer, particularly in patients with cancer of the breast. Some surgeons believe that if the disease is treated early in its course, the cancer should be removed but the lymphatic glands in the armpit should be spared for they will filter off and destroy any cells which escape from the cancer at operation. Others hold that the glands should always be removed for they are frequently the site of secondary deposits often too small to be seen with the naked eye. The fact that no agreement has been reached and that the argument continues to rage after many years suggests that neither approach has much advantage over the other.

That the problems of metastasis in cancer are many and unsolved has already been mentioned. There are many instances in which the primary growth can be adequately treated, but the presence of metastases prove the cancer to be incurable. Frequently metastases will make their appearance shortly after the primary cancer has apparently been 'cured'. There have been rare occasions on which widespread metastasis has followed operation so rapidly that it has been suggested that surgery was in some way responsible for the dissemination. The presence of secondary deposits, however, no longer carried quite such a dismal outlook as it did. There are occasions when excision of a single solitary metastasis after the primary tumour has been removed has resulted in cure. Sometimes radiotherapy or chemotherapy can deal with them adequately. Nevertheless it remains true that the discovery of secondary deposits usually makes the chances of cure remote.

The physical features of cancers are as variable as their other characteristics. They usually present as tumours— swellings appreciable to the examining hand. The tumour is irregular in shape, hard, and feels as if anchored to the underlying tissues. If it arises on a surface it may infiltrate the overlying skin or mucous membrane, destroy it, and give rise to an ulcer. When arising in a tube-like structure such as the bowel it may spread round its circumference to form a ring which reduces its calibre. In the breast it is usually felt as an irregular mass.

The pathologist has a classification of cancers which is founded upon the tissue from which they arise. There are two main divisions. The first type are those which arise from epithelium, a term which includes the skin, mucous membranes and most of the glands other than the lymphatic glands (which are strictly speaking not glands at all). Tumours arising from epithelium are carcinomas; those of glandular origin are called adenocarcinomas. Those arising from skin or mucous membrane are often qualified by the type of cell from which they spring: thus, there are squamous-cell, basal-cell, or transitional-cell carcinomas. The second major division consists of those tumours which spring from the connective tissue – the supporting tissues of the body. These are known as sarcomas and again are qualified by a prefix which shows their origin: thus the fibrosarcoma arises from fibrous tissue, the osteosarcoma from bone, and the lymphosarcoma from lymphatic tissue. Teratomas are rare tumours thought to develop from cells normally existing in the embryo which have usually disappeared by the time the foetus is fully developed. They usually occur in childhood and are often of rapid growth.

Many attempts have been made to grade cancers by their

microscopic appearances in the belief that this would provide a guide to the degree of malignancy. It has proved a difficult exercise and an uncertain guide to the tumour's behaviour. So many variables exist in human cancer, some in the nature of the tumour and some in the patient in whom the tumour appears, that it is unlikely that the single characteristic of cellular appearance will provide a dependable yardstick by which to predict the outcome.

4

Some figures

The human race may be divided into those for whom statistics possess a peculiar fascination and those in whom they arouse sensations of paralysing ennui. This chapter is addressed to those in the first category and members of the second are advised to avert their gaze and rapidly turn the pages. Whatever views we hold, statistics supply the raw material from which we can measure the size of the problem cancer presents and its impact upon the nation's health. They furnish the information upon which the results of treatment are assessed. Changes in the numbers of persons affected, variations in the incidence of the disease in different countries, in the ages at which it is most common, and in the proportions of men an women it attacks all provide clues which may help in identifying a cause. No-one with an interest in the broader aspects of cancer can afford to neglect statistics however unappetizing he may find them. Andrew Lang once observed of a writer, 'he uses statistics as a drunken man uses lamp-posts—for support rather than illumination'. It is in the hope of illuminating some of the darkness which surrounds malignant disease that this chapter is written.

For many years now in this country the cause of death has had to be notified to the Registrar of Births and Deaths; the figures are collated, analysed, and published by the Office of Population Censuses and Surveys, formerly known as the General Registry Office. From these the mortality of cancer, or the number of persons dying from the disease can be derived. It is more important, however, to know how many persons develop cancer in each year, that is, its incidence. Since 1962 the whole of England, Wales, and Scotland has been covered by 'cancer registries' to which all persons in whom a diagnosis of cancer is made in National Health

23

Service hospitals are notified. The management of these registries is the responsibility of the Department of Health and Social Security in England and Wales and the Home and Health Department in Scotland.

The accuracy of the figures derived from death certificates as well as those from cancer notifications has been questioned. The first are reasonably dependable: all deaths are notified, although in some instances the cause may be uncertain. Nevertheless, the records represent the most accurate that can be obtained and it is likely that errors are becoming progressively less frequent. The figures drawn from the cancer registries are less trustworthy. Some patients with cancer may not be admitted to a National Health Service hospital, sometimes registration is overlooked, and sometimes, when there are frequent admissions to hospital, a case is notified more than once. A final difficulty lies in the labels attached to the individual forms of cancer. An International Classification of Diseases is published at intervals of ten years; the last edition, the ninth, came into effect early in 1979. This classification is used in all the published statistical tables, but changes are often made between editions and the figures for one period may on this account not be comparable with those of another. In spite of the potential sources of error, both the figures for mortality and those for incidence or morbidity are of great value to the research workers in cancer as well as to those concerned with the health of the public.

Before discussing some of the figures available, it should be explained how the results are expressed. The 'mortality' is the total number of persons dying from the disease in question for the year or years under review; sexes are commonly considered separately. The 'mortality rate' or 'death rate' is the number of persons dying of the disease in question per year per 1 000 000 living. When the death rate refers to persons of a given age – for example, those aged 45–54 years – it is stated as the number of deaths per 1 000 000 living persons of that age. Similarly figures for 'incidence' or

Some figures

'morbidity' are given as total numbers of persons notified as suffering from the disease in question within the period under review, or as the registration rate per year per 1 000 000 persons living. All the figures given in this chapter refer to England and Wales unless otherwise stated and when the unqualified terms 'mortality rate' or 'incidence' are used to the number of persons per 1 000 000 living per year.

The numbers certified as dying from cancer in England and Wales in 1975, the last year for which figures are available, are to be found in Table 1. For purposes of comparison the number of deaths from cardiovascular disease is appended. Over the years the numbers dying of cancer have increased sharply. In the 5 years 1911–15 the total deaths and, in parentheses, the death rates from this disease per 1 000 000 living were males 87 929 (992) and females 115 125 (1216).

Table 1: *Deaths from cancer in England and Wales in 1975*

	Males	Females	Total
Number of persons dying from all causes	294 174	288 667	582 841
Number of persons dying from cancer	65 791	56 658	122 449
Number of deaths from cancer as percentage of all deaths	22.4	19.6	21
Number of persons dying from cancer per 1 000 000 living	2769	2271	
Number of persons dying from cardiovascular diseases*	115 039	117 525	232 564
Number of deaths from cardiovascular disease as percentage of all deaths	39.1	40.7	39.9

*Diseases of the heart and arteries and strokes.

It will be noted that then more women died of cancer than men. For the 5-year period 1966–70 the figures were 307 035 (2620) males and 261 037 (2100) females. The total number

25

of males dying had increased 3·5 times and the death rate 2·5 times. The increase in women dying was less, the figures for the second period being 2¼ and 1¾ times those of the first. Male deaths now preponderate over female largely due to the increased number of men dying from cancer of the lung. In the period 1941–5 19 900 more men than women died from this cause: 25 years later from 1966–1970 the excess of male deaths had risen to 95 425.

The figures for the general incidence of cancer are, for reasons already explained, less dependable than those for mortality. Some representative figures are set out in Table 2. It will be seen that the incidence in England and Wales differs little from the rates in other industrialized western countries, but in those countries where the standard of living is lower, the recorded incidence is also lower. This difference can perhaps be explained partly by less well-developed medical services and thus less accurate diagnosis and registration. It is also likely that in countries where the average expectation of life is low fewer persons live to an age at which cancer becomes common. There are only a few rare forms of cancer in which the incidence rate does not increase with age.

Table 2. *Registered incidence of cancer in various countries*

(Numbers of persons certified as affected per million living)

Country	Males	Females
England and Wales	2545	1963
United States of America	2578	2200
Germany	2444	2166
Denmark	2221	2000
New Zealand (Europeans)	2421	2233
India	1395	1311
Nigeria	767	1048

Many changes in mortality and incidence of cancer have been noted over the past half century and some of these, affecting the commoner types, deserve discussion. It is not possible because of the alteration in nomenclature to compare figures for all cancers over the 50-year period.

Cancer of the lip, mouth, and tongue have become progressively less common. For example, the mortality rate of cancer of the tongue in men fell from 53 to 9 between the quinquennia 1911–1915 and 1966–1970. In women is was unchanged remaining at the low figure of 5. It has been suggested that the smoking of pipes and cigars plays some part in its cause. Cancer of the gullet (oesophagus) became more common in men between the quinquennia 1911–15 and 1936–40, then declined and has now risen again to 79 in 1975. In women, however, the death rate per year per 1 000 000 living rose from 20 for 1911–15 to 50 for 1966–70, and to 59 in 1975. In men it is unduly common in the Liverpool and Manchester areas; in women it is more common in Wales. This may be linked with anaemia due to lack of iron known to be especially frequent in Cardiff and to be associated with precancerous changes at the upper end of the gullet. Throughout the world the incidence of cancer of the oesophagus shows strange differences. These have been attributed to variations in the use of tobacco and alcohol, but this is not an adequate explanation. Allusion has been made in Chapter 2 to the high incidence of this disease in a province of Iran bordering the Caspian Sea, where the incidence rate is 1100 in men and 1840 in women. The inhabitants of this area take no alcohol.

The death rate from cancer of the stomach shows curious changes and geographical variations. In both men and women this disease became more common between the 5-year periods 1911–15 and 1951–55, the death rate rising in men from 201 to 378, and then falling for 1966–70 to 314, a reduction of 17 per cent. In women the rise was from 171 to 278 for the 5 years 1946–50, with a fall to 222 for the 5-year period 1966–70, a drop of 20 per cent. By 1975 further falls were recorded, in men to 291 and women to 198. Cancer of the stomach is especially common in Japan where the rate of incidence is about 950 per 1 000 000 living. It has been reported that in immigrants to Japan the incidence of cancer of the stomach increases to levels similar to those of the indigenous population. This suggests that an environmental carcinogen is important and genetic factors less so. It seems likely, however, that those who are of blood group A are more likely to develop cancer of the stomach: thus, there is probably some genetic influence.

Cancers of the large bowel and the rectum present several points of interest. First those of the large bowel are 1·5 times (1:1·5) more common in women than in men, while those of the rectum are slightly more common in men (1:0·9). In both sexes the death rates for cancer of the colon rose from 1931 to 1935 to reach peaks between 1941 and 1950, then fall again for the quinquennium 1966–70. They appear to be rising once more and the rates for 1975 were for men 177 and women 248. Cancer of the rectum follows the same pattern; the 1975 rates were 135 in males and 113 in females. There is a high incidence of cancer of the large bowel in Western Scotland which has not been explained and a lesser excess in south-east England, while more cases than expected are registered in the west Midlands.

An unexplained increase has been noted in the deaths reported as due to cancer of the pancreas, a gland which provides the digestive juices and lies on the back wall of the abdomen. Because diagnosis is often difficult and thus usually late, effective treatment is seldom possible and the mortality and morbidity rate differ little. For the quinquennium 1911–15 the death rate per 1 000 000 living was 18 for males and 16 for females. For the period 1966–70 the rates had risen to 110 and 92—more than a fivefold increase. The figures for 1975 show further increase and are males 124 and females 103. There is no clue to the cause of this remarkable change, although an association with cigarette smoking has been suggested. Cancer of the pancreas is particularly common in south-east England.

The increased incidence of cancer of the lung is familiar to everyone. Figures before 1941 are not available because of changes in nomenclature, but the record since then shows

Some figures

the trend. For the 5-year period 1941–5 the death rate in men was 260 and in women 60, by 1966–70 the rates had risen to 1025 and 199, increases of 294 per cent and 234 per cent. For 1975 the death rate in men was 1089 and in women 269. In this year in England and Wales 26 294 men and women died from cancer of the lung, 33 140 persons, a number amounting to 5.7 per cent of all recorded deaths. Thus more than 1 death in every 20 is due to cancer of the lung. The disease in men is more common in the north-west, west Midlands, and south-east England: in women it is more frequent in the south and south-east.

Cancer of the breast is the commonest form of malignant disease in women, and its frequency is increasing. The death rate for the 5 years 1911–15 was 198 per 1 000 000 living, by 1966–70 it had risen to 415 and for the year 1975 it was 461. In this year 11 637 women died of this disease. It is registered most frequently in the west Midlands and south-east England. There are curious geographical variations. Its rarity in Japanese women has already been noted: in that country the death rate is 111. It is of interest that Japanese when they emigrate become no more susceptible to cancer of the breast and thus the cause for their relative freedom from the disease is likely to be genetic, although cultural differences may have some influence.

Cancer of the cervix or neck of the womb has a particular importance for it is one of the few cancers for which preventive measures believed to be efficacious are available. They are discussed in Chapter 6. Unfortunately, a change in the nomenclature has made comparison with figures before the quinquennium 1951–5 valueless. For this 5-year period the death rate was 109 per 1 000 000 living; by the period 1966–70 it had fallen by 12 per cent to 98 and in 1975 it had decreased further to 85. It remains more common in northern England than in the rest of the country.

Cancer of the ovary is another tumour which has become a more common cause of death in the last half-century. In the quinquennium 1911–15 the death rate was 28, by

29

1966–70 it had risen to 139, and for the year 1975 it was 144. Thus the numbers have increased fivefold. It has been suggested that improvements in diagnosis explain this rise, but it is unlikely to be the sole cause. In Great Britain the incidence is highest in the West Midlands and the South East. A strange and unexplained variation occurs in Jewish women: in those born in Europe or the United States the morbidity rate is 153, but in those born in Israel it is only 73.

The incidence of cancer of the prostate continues to increase; for the period 1911–15 the death rate was only 25 per 1 000 000 living, for 1966–70 it was 168, and for the year 1975 it was 184. This represents a 7.5-fold increase. It can be accounted for largely by two factors. First, diagnosis has become more precise. It is a disease which is often latent and discovered only on microscopic study. Secondly, it becomes progressively more common as the years advance, thus with the increasing age of the population the potential number of sufferers also increases.

Cancer of the bladder occurs twice as commonly in men as in women. The death rate has risen steadily over the last 50 years. For the period 1911–15 it was 88 per 1 000 000 living for men and 35 for women; for 1966–70, 111 for men and 44 for women; and for the year 1975, 118 and 49 respectively. It seems probable that an external carcinogen is responsible. It is easy to understand how potentially harmful waste products excreted and concentrated in the urine made by the kidney could act on the mucous membrane lining the bladder. Certain chemicals formerly used in the dye-stuffs and rubber industries are recognized causes of bladder cancer and there is an established link with cigarette smoking. Its association with bilharziasis (schistosomiasis) in Egypt and other countries where this infection is rife has been discussed in Chapter 2.

Brain tumours differ from the varieties already considered. Many primary growths of the brain and spinal cord are not malignant in the full meaning of the term. They infiltrate the surrounding tissue, but they do not give rise to secondary deposits; indeed, a number are benign in the sense the word is used by pathologists. They cause serious symptoms because they grow in a confined space, either within the skull or the spinal canal. The earlier figures for the number of deaths certified as due to 'malignant neoplasms' of the brain and central nervous system are thus of questionable accuracy. For the period 1941–5 the death rate was 23 per 1 000 000 living in men and 15 in women. There was a sudden sharp increase during the 1950s and for 1966–70 the figures were 49 and 33. They have changed little since, being 51 and 35 for 1975. Diagnostic accuracy improved greatly during these years and it is possible that some brain tumours certified as primary were secondary deposits from cancer of the lung. Such metastases, often in the absence of cough or other lung symptoms, are common.

The final group of cancers to be considered are those which arise in lymphatic glands or from the related cells in the organs which form the blood. The commonest of the first group is Hodgkin's disease. Although rare, 744 persons were certified as dying from it in 1975, it has a disproportionate importance for the student of cancer because it has proved curable by treatments other than surgical. Precise diagnosis is completely dependent on the microscopic examination of excised tissue by an experienced pathologist. In the earlier years its accuracy was questionable. The numbers per 1 000 000 living certified as dying from Hodgkin's disease in the period 1911–15 were 10 men and 6 women. For 1966–70 they were 23 and 14. For the year 1975 they were 19 and 11. This fall probably reflects the efficacy of treatment over the past few years.

The second group, leukaemia, is numerically small, but again of great interest to the research worker in the field of cancer. In the year 1975 it caused 3194 deaths in England and Wales. The term leukaemia covers a number of related diseases, the diagnosis of which requires considerable expertise. The individual types may well have different causes, they certainly differ in their age, sex, and geographical incidence. These points are discussed in a later chapter and the following figures refer to all forms of the disease. The death rates for the quinquennium 1911–15 were 12 for males and 10 for females. For 1966–70 they had risen to 69 and 55, and for the year 1975 further rises to 73 and 57 are recorded. Some of the increase is due to improved diagnosis but it seems certain that there has been a true increase in the incidence of this disease.

In this chapter certain statistical aspects of the cancer problem have been discussed. The points which emerge are first that the total number of persons dying from cancer has increased. When the two 5-year periods 1911–15 and 1966–70 are compared, the number of deaths for the first was 203 054 and for the second 568 072, an increase of 280 per cent. The number of deaths from cancer per year per 1 000 000 living was 1107 and 2352, a rise of 212 per cent. In 1975 one-fifth of all deaths were due to this cause. At any rate in part this remarkable rise can be explained by the increasing longevity of the population, which brings more and more people into the age at which cancer is most common. This in its turn is due to improvement in the health of the nation's youth and to the conquest of infection by the antibiotic drugs. When individual forms of the disease are considered it will be seen that some, such as cancer of the lung, have become commoner for reasons which are identifiable; some, like cancer of the pancreas, have become inexplicably commoner; and some, like cancer of the stomach, have become less common.

The common forms of cancer in 1975, judged by the frequency with which they are certified as the cause of death, are shown in Table 3, the figure after each being the death rate for the disease in question stated as a percentage of the total number of persons of that sex certified as dying from cancer in the year.

It will have been noted that almost all the figures refer to numbers of deaths and death rates. It must not be concluded from this that cancer is inevitably fatal. These are the only

Some figures

dependable figures in existence. The work of the cancer registries is only a few years old; the records of deaths due to this disease extend back for a century and are of necessity more accurate. These figures give the only available guide to the frequency of cancer, and of the sex and age incidence. They must, of course, be accepted with reservation. When full and dependable figures for incidence are available for an extended period, the picture may well be found to be different. It is known, for example, that many cancers of the breast and colon are cured and that only a small percentage of cancers of the skin prove fatal. Nevertheless, the figures for mortality and mortality rates reveal only too clearly the immensity of the problem facing workers in the field of cancer.

Table 3. *Death rates for the common forms of cancer, stated as the percentage of the total dying from cancer in the year (1975)*

Males		Females	
Lung	39.2	Breast	20.3
Stomach	10.5	Lung	11.8
Prostate	6.6	Colon	10.9
Colon	6.3	Stomach	8.7
Leukaemia and		Ovary	6.3
lymphoma	6.0	Leukaemia and	
Rectum	4.5	lymphoma	6.0
Pancreas	4.5	Rectum	4.6
Bladder	4.3	Pancreas	4.5
		Cervix	3.7
		Bladder	2.1

5

Symptoms

There are no symptoms which can be regarded as typical of cancer. Indeed, it is clear that the kind of illness it causes must depend largely upon the region in which the tumour arises. In the early stages health is usually unimpaired, although the word 'early' must be used with caution for there is always a stage of unknown duration in which the cancer could only be recognized on microscopic examination of the affected organ. 'Early' means no more than that the tumour has reached a size at which it can just be detected and this varies greatly with its situation. Nevertheless while many have no symptoms at this stage, others are conscious of a vague ill-health before any recognizable signs of cancer appear. These symptoms are often dismissed as trivial: they include such mundane complaints as being 'off colour' and lack of the customary *joie de vivre*; appetite may be less sharp and there may be some loss of weight; occasionally there is even a little rise in temperature. They often seem so minor and ill-defined that they do not warrant a visit to the doctor, but they should be taken seriously if they persist.

The first outward and visible sign of cancer again depends upon the organ or tissue from which it arises. If it is on the surface of the body, for example in the breast, it will show itself as a swelling which may be visible and cause some change in contour or may only be felt with the hand. A cancerous swelling is hard; it is usually painless and it is not tender. At this stage advice is ordinarily sought, but if it is neglected and the tumour is allowed to progress untreated it will increase in size and, because cancers spread by infiltration, it will come to feel fixed as though anchored to the tissues beneath it. If it spreads towards the surface the skin

34

will become attached to it and may later be destroyed to leave a malignant ulcer which slowly spreads. For many centuries the word 'cancer' meant a creeping ulcer of this type and for long it was the form cancer often took. It is now of great rarity and is only seen in those who have refused or been unable to obtain treatment at an earlier stage.

A cancer arising in the bowel, stomach, or bladder behaves in a similar way, destroying the lining mucous membrane and leading to ulceration. From this raw ulcerated surface bleeding may occur and vomiting of blood or its presence in the motion or the urine is often an early symptom of cancer of one of these organs. Sometimes the spread is outwards and the cancer may destroy the outer coat of the bowel, leaving a track by which its contents may escape, to give rise to peritonitis, inflammation of the lining of the abdominal cavity.

There are many organs in the body which are hollow and tube-like. Examples are the intestines, the gullet or oesophagus, the air-passages or bronchi, and the ducts which carry the urine from the kidney to the bladder or the bile from the liver to the bowel. Cancers arising in these will often lead to narrowing of the calibre or even actual blockage of the tube. Thus difficulty in swallowing and a sensation of food being held up at some point in the gullet is an early symptom of cancer of the oesophagus. With cancer of the large intestine some change from the normal regular rhythm of evacuation is often the first warning. It may be increasing constipation, diarrhoea alternating with periods of constipation, or even a complete blockage of the bowel which draws attention to the trouble. In the bronchi an irritating cough is often the first complaint. When the cancer has caused an ulcer of the lining membrane of one of the air-tubes, a little blood may be coughed up. This symptom, for many years almost diagnostic of consumption, is now far more often the first indication of cancer of the lung. If an air-tube is narrowed or blocked by the tumour, the phlegm which is normally coughed up accumulates behind the narrowed area, becomes invaded by microbes and an illness resembling pneumonia results.

Any hollow tube may also be blocked by pressure from a tumour growing outside it. Cancer of the lung may press upon neighbouring air tubes or upon the large veins within the chest. This will lead to distension of veins in the neck or even to swelling of the neck itself and an early complaint may be of the collar being uncomfortably tight. Similarly the bile duct which carries the bile from the liver to the intestine may be blocked by pressure from without. A common cause is cancer of the pancreas, a gland concerned with digestion lying deep within the abdomen. The bile, prevented from reaching the intestine, seeps back into the blood giving the skin and eyes the yellow colour known as jaundice. Cancer of the bladder may lead to blockage of the ureter, the duct through which urine passes from the kidney to the bladder. Usually only one ureter is obstructed and the kidney on that side will be prevented from working.

A tumour may, even when it is small, interfere with the proper working of an organ. Cancer of the throat, especially when it arises from one of the vocal cords, is an illustration: it leads to hoarseness early in its course. In like fashion a small growth in the eye soon causes some disturbance of sight.

It is difficult to explode the myth that cancer is inevitably painful. It cannot be denied that the disease may cause pain and sometimes intense pain. When this occurs it is usually in the later stages of cancers which have proved incurable and then in probably less than half those it affects. Pain is rare early in its course and in some forms it is exceptional. It may be caused by pressure on nerves in the neighbourhood of the tumour, but more often it is due to the cancer spreading to infiltrate the neighbouring tissues and the nerves they contain. It is often a problem when the organ from which it arises is one in constant movement, thus the tongue, the mouth, and the upper part of the throat are areas in which small cancers are often painful. Severe pain is perhaps most

36

often due to secondary deposits, rather than to the primary tumour: this is especially true of secondary deposits in bones.

Other symptoms arise which are not directly caused by the primary cancer. These are of two varieties: first, those due to metastases or secondary deposits and secondly various bizarre symptoms probably caused by substances made by the tumour cells. The mechanism by which metastases arise are discussed in Chapter 3.

There are certain organs in which metastases, especially when they are blood-borne, are particularly likely to arise. First amongst these is the liver. It is the largest organ in the body and has a copious blood supply so that the cancer cells in the blood stream are likely to lodge in its network of blood vessels which acts like a filter. Metastases in the liver often lead to great enlargement of the organ with discomfort or pain below the ribs on the right and in the flank. There may be jaundice from interference with the drainage of bile and less often other symptoms of liver disease such as irrition of the skin, twitching, and drowsiness.

Perhaps the second commonest site for metastases is the lung. Here again the amount of blood flowing through the organ must increase the probability of cancer cells circulating in it finding a resting place. Such secondary deposits do not always cause symptoms. If they are near the surface of the lung a pain like that of pleurisy results. In some patients fluid forms within the chest and shortness of breath becomes troublesome, a symptom also likely to arise when there are many metastases scattered throughout the lungs.

There are few tissues or organs in which secondary deposits may not be found. Of particular consequence are the brain, the skin, and the bones. The importance of the first is obvious. Such secondary deposits are particularly common when the lung is the seat of a primary cancer, which is sometimes so small that it eludes detection and the symptoms are wrongly attributed to a primary brain tumour. These metastases declare themselves early because they expand within the rigid confines of the skull.

Small nodules, often not more than three or four milli-metres in diameter, may occur in the skin. Their discovery may enable a diagnosis which has long been in doubt to be established. They are perhaps most common in patients with cancer of the breast, but may be seen with malignant melan-oma, an uncommon malignant mole, and many other forms of cancer.

It is still unknown why some cancers have a particular tendency to metastasize in the skeleton. The problem is discussed in Chapter 3. The varieties with this peculiar pro-pensity are those arising in the breast, the prostate, the lung, the stomach, the thyroid gland, and the kidney. Secondary deposits occur in two forms: first as a solitary metastatic tumour which weakens and may finally destroy an area of bone, and secondly as a general spread throughout the bone marrow and the outer part of the bone as well.

The first may result in a bone giving way at the point where the metastasis has weakened it, often as a result of some trivial injury or strain, sometimes without any apparent cause. This is termed a spontaneous or pathological fracture. Sometimes the secondary deposit is in one of the vertebrae of the spine and this too may give way suddenly, collapsing under the weight it is normally called upon to carry. Vertebral collapse is usually accompanied by intense pain and some-times leads to pressure upon the spinal cord causing paralysis of the legs. This solitary type of metastasis is seen most frequently with cancers arising in the breast, thyroid, and kidney, although the primary tumour may be found in almost any organ. Sometimes one will appear early in the course of the disease and a pathological fracture may be the first indication of the presence of cancer.

The second type of bony metastasis is seen particularly in patients with cancer of the prostate, but is not uncommon when the primary tumour is in the breast, lung, or stomach. Here the spread is often in the bone-marrow rather than the solid outer part or cortex of the bone. When the cortex is also affected the bone often becomes unduly hard and appears abnormally opaque to X-rays. Pain is often trivial or even absent. The disease spreads gradually throughout the marrow of the bones particularly of the spine, the ribs, and the pelvis. The bone marrow is the factory of the cells of the blood and in consequence those with metastases of this kind are usually anaemic because the cancer has destroyed the blood-making tissues. In cancer of the prostate especially, where the primary tumour often causes trivial symptoms, the first complaints may be those of anaemia: shortness of breath, exhaustion, and palpitation of the heart.

It should be added that secondary deposits in the bones usually give rise to pain. It has already been pointed out that when a metastasis causes collapse of a vertebra pain is often of great intensity. Pain is a particular feature of the solitary type of metastasis even in the absence of a pathological fracture, although this complication inevitably makes it worse. Characteristically it is at its worst during the night hours. In the second type of metastasis where the marrow of the bones is infiltrated by cancer, pain is not a feature and pathological fractures are exceptional. A generalized aching, often thought to be rheumatic, is common and the complaint is usually of backache.

Secondary deposits become increasingly common the longer the cancer has been in existence, but they may form early in its course. Indeed, it is not uncommon for the appearance of metastases to be the cause of the initial symptoms and it may be difficult or even impossible to discern the site of the primary tumour. The early occurrence of a secondary deposit in the brain has already been noted. More common are metastases in the liver which lead to pain under the ribs on the right and may arise early in the course of cancers of the bowel or pancreas before the primary tumour has given rise to any symptoms. The same is true of both types of metastasis in bones.

The second way in which cancer spreads to other areas, lymphatic spread, has been discussed in Chapter 3. Usually the extension takes place in a regular orderly fashion: the glands first affected are those nearest the primary tumour normally concerned with draining the lymph from the area in which it is situated. From these the growth extends to the next anatomically related group and there the process continues. The lymphatic gland which is the seat of a metastasis has characters similar to those of a primary cancer: it is hard, painless at first, and when the cancer has broken through the outer covering of the gland it will be fixed to the tissues in its neighbourhood. This lymphatic spread increases in extent with the advance of the primary tumour, but here, as with other metastases, an enlarged lymphatic gland may be the first sign of the disease. This may be so with cancer of the breast when the glands in one armpit are affected. More often perhaps a small primary tumour in the region of the tonsil or at the back of the throat declares itself by enlarged lymphatic glands on one or other side of the neck. It is only when a meticulous search is made that the primary tumour is discovered. Cancer of the lung spreads to the glands lying deep in the chest behind the breast bone and these may grow to form a large tumour which comes to press upon nerves and veins in its vicinity.

In addition to blood-borne metastasis and lymphatic spread, cancer can give rise to other symptoms remote from the primary growth. The explanation for some of these is uncertain. The first group of these are of endocrine origin. There are a number of glands in the body normally engaged in making substances known as hormones which they pour into the circulating blood and which have a profound effect upon the body's activities. These are the endocrine glands and a familiar example is the thyroid gland making the hormone thyroxine. The amounts made are regulated by a complex system of checks and balances to correspond with the body's requirements. Sometimes cancers arise the cells of which possess the capacity for making a hormone, although the cancer is not derived from the endocrine gland normally responsible for it. The tumour most often endowed with this curious property is cancer of the lung. Many examples have been reported where such a neoplasm has the ability to make a substance with an action like a hormone of the pituitary gland and others in which the product acts like that of the parathyroid glands. The patient will seek advice for symptoms which suggest overactivity of one or other of the endocrine glands. It is only after prolonged investigation that the cause is found to be a cancer, probably with none of the characteristic symptoms, which has the power of making a hormone-like substance.

The second group consists of those whose initial complaints suggest some nervous or muscular disease. This may be no more than simple, but excessive, muscular weakness, combined perhaps with odd sensations such as pins and needles or numbness of the fingers or toes. Occasionally there may be actual paralysis of muscles or signs which indicate disease of the brain or spinal cord. In many cases these symptoms do not fit in with any of the well-recognized patterns of illness and it is only after full investigation that a primary tumour is discovered. This may be in the stomach, but as in the case of other bizarre symptoms, it is most frequently a cancer of the lung.

The final group is of certain skin diseases which appear to be connected with cancer. The nature of this connection is unknown, but they occur far more often in those with cancer than in those without and in some the association is virtually constant. Common symptoms are generalized itching, and dryness and scaliness of the skin. These can be described as 'non-specific' for although they often appear in association with cancer they are not uncommon without any clear cause. There is a group of skin diseases called acanthosis nigricans; in one form and particularly in the middle-aged it is almost always associated with cancer of the stomach or ovary. It is shown by a dark, almost black, warty thickening of the skin especially in the armpits. Another association is between an inflammation of the skin and underlying muscles known as dermatomyositis. This affects the skin of the face, upper part of the chest and the forearms, and the muscles

41

in those areas. After middle age this condition is accompanied by cancer in at least half in those in whom it develops.

Many of the strange symptoms just described are rare and in the great majority of those who develop cancer the disease runs a constant and predictable course. They are noted here because they have considerable scientific interest and because they can often cause confusion and delay in discovering the underlying cancer.

In the great majority there is a preliminary period of vague ill-health rapidly succeeded by a phase in which the symptoms are those of the primary tumour. These, of course, vary with the organ from which it springs. In favourable cases appropriate treatment at this stage removes the primary tumour, symptoms disappear and there is complete and permanent recovery. If the primary tumour for some reason cannot be removed or adequately treated it will extend locally causing destruction of tissues in its neighbourhood and perhaps symptoms due to pressure on nerves, blood vessels, and other structures. In many a stage of dissemination follows in which blood-borne metastases occur and there is spread to the lymphatic glands. Sometimes metastases too small to see have taken place before treatment of the primary tumour has been undertaken; then, however successful this seems to have been, after a while secondary deposits will make their appearance. The interval before these microscopic metastases become evident is strangely variable: in the great majority it is within five years, but occasionally they appear after as long as 20 years of seemingly unimpaired health.

In a growing number it is becoming possible to slow down, arrest, and sometimes perhaps cure the cancerous process even when dissemination has taken place. Sadly there remains a considerable proportion in which the disease progresses inexorably. With this advance the patient may pass into a state known as 'cachexia'. This is a picture only too familiar to the doctor and one which remains indelibly imprinted on the minds of many who have watched relatives die of cancer. Appetite fails, weight is lost, and muscular weakness becomes

Symptoms

overwhelming. The skin loses its normal elasticity, becoming pallid, dry and parchment-like; the hair is lank and without lustre; the eyes are dull and sunken. Unable to leave his bed, he will often be apathetic and uninterested in his surroundings, isolated in a little world of his own which is penetrated only with difficulty. Pain, nausea, inability to eat, the results of infection, overenthusiastic dosage with pain-killing drugs and gradual failure of many of the vital organs account for much of this, combined with the indignities of dependence and an overwhelming sense of loneliness. Happily this picture is becoming rare. Sympathetic and informed care can illuminate the last days of the patient with cancer and give them peace and dignity.

6

Diagnosis

In cancer diagnosis entails much more than merely affixing a label. The word needs to be given its full meaning of a 'thorough perception or knowledge' of the illness which afflicts the patient. It is important for the doctor to know where the primary cancer has arisen, its exact nature as revealed by the microscope, and whether it has remained localized, spread to the lymphatic glands in its neighbourhood, or given rise to blood-borne secondary deposits. Only when all this information is available can a rational plan for treatment be designed. This chapter of necessity contains much technical matter which might be regarded as the province of the doctor alone. Nevertheless it is important to dispel the aura of mystery which surrounds the diagnostic process. For this reason those who are potential patients should be able to understand what the doctor is trying to do and the problems which face him. Without such knowledge the co-operation between doctor and patient essential to good treatment cannot be achieved.

The earlier the diagnosis of cancer is made and treatment instituted the more favourable the outlook. A tumour will cause symptoms only after it has been growing for some time and clearly its detection before symptoms arose would be an advantage. In the hopes of achieving this aim regular examinations of the apparently healthy have their advocates. This procedure, known as 'screening', is discussed in Chapter 7. Efforts to detect cancer in this early stage lead logically to examination for precancerous changes and this to avoidance of the recognizable causes of cancer. This chapter is concerned with the diagnosis of cancer in patients who have symptoms or signs which suggest its presence.

It cannot be stressed too forcibly that a diagnosis of cancer demands proof wherever this is possible and that proof requires microscopic examination of the suspected tissue by a skilled pathologist. Until this has been done the diagnosis may be assumed with varying degrees of suspicion, but can never be regarded as proven. Before such an examination can be made, tissue has to be available. This is easy enough when the tumour is accessible and a fragment can be removed by the surgeon. This minor diagnostic procedure is known as a *'biopsy'*. When no biopsy is possible, material from the tumour may sometimes be obtained with a needle or a more extensive operation may be necessary. A tumour within the abdomen is an example: X-ray studies may show that it is likely to be a cancer, but it is impossible to obtain tissue for the pathologist to examine. In these circumstances an operation is essential at which the diagnosis can be confirmed and the surgeon can proceed forthwith to remove the tumour.

The symptoms of ill-health to which malignant disease may give rise are described in Chapter 5. Here it is only necessary to repeat that they are frequently ill-defined and early in the course of the disease may consist of little more than such indeterminate complaints as lethargy, distaste for food, and loss of weight. Accompanying these or arising without disturbance of general health may be one or more symptoms which throw suspicion on a single organ or system, the sudden onset of cough with spitting of blood would be an example. The doctor therefore needs constantly to bear in mind the possibility that his patient may have cancer and that it is his duty to reach a diagnosis as early as possible, but at the same time that he must avoid arousing alarm and apprehension which may later prove unfounded.

The next step in the process of diagnosis lies in physical examination. The doctor may find some abnormality which supports the suspicions the symptoms have aroused. It may point unequivocally to a particular organ or it may provide evidence of widespread disease. Often, however, physical examination reveals no abnormality and then the question of further investigation arises. In these circumstances the doctor has to decide what is justifiable. No-one would wish to expose every patient to all the investigations required to exclude the presence of cancer. First, it is clear that it is impossible to be certain that no cancer exists, for at an early stage only a microscopic examination could detect it. Secondly, in this situation as in many others it is impossible to prove a negative. The doctor alone is in a position to judge whether the degree of suspicion is sufficient to justify further tests.

The form such tests should take depends upon whether the symptoms are only those of general ill-health or whether suspicion falls on one particular organ or region of the body. In the first instance, there are various blood tests which, if positive, would do little more than reinforce the suspicion that all was not well. If they prove normal in one whose symptoms are vague and in whom examination has disclosed no signs of disease, it is usual to take things no further. If they are abnormal and support the view that something is amiss, other tests will be required, their nature depending upon circumstances. If there are symptoms which indicate disease in one particular area, the tests must be those which aim to reveal abnormalities in the area under suspicion.

Advances in medical technology have immensely increased the ability to detect disease in an early stage and the various devices which are useful in the diagnosis of cancer are many. It has already been explained that diagnosis must be incontrovertible and to ensure this the microscopic examination of tissue from the suspected tumour is essential. The first group of techniques are those which allow specimens to be obtained from normally inaccessible sites. A number of instruments have been designed which allow the operator to inspect parts of the body's interior. These are spoken of as 'endoscopes'. For many years they have been available for examination of the urinary bladder (cystoscope), gullet (oesophagoscope), and many other areas. Through them the lining membranes can be examined, cancers or ulcers identified, and a fragment of the diseased area removed for the pathologist to examine. This is the routine method of establishing a diagnosis of cancer of any of these organs before radical treatment is undertaken. The surface of the liver can be inspected through a peritoneoscope, and the presence of metastases confirmed. This instrument allows too the inspection of the outer coat of the bowel where secondary deposits may be seen. In some centres a culdoscope is used to inspect the womb and ovaries: it is passed through a small incision in the vagina. Over the last 10 years a flexible endoscope has been devised which makes use of the fibre-optic principle and allows the operator to 'look round corners' and obtain an excellent view even when the instrument is bent at a right angle. This has made possible inspection and examination of areas of the body which were previously inaccessible. The mucous membrane lining the entire stomach and the duodenum, the area of intestine immediately beyond it, are now open to endoscopic examination and the same is true of the large bowel where early cancers and precancerous states can be identified and samples obtained for microscopic examination. It is because they permit biopsies from areas which cannot ordinarily be reached that these new endoscopic methods are so valuable.

In addition to biopsy of the type described, a firm diagnosis may sometimes be made without even this minor operation. Many superficial cancers shed cells from their surfaces or they can be obtained by gentle swabbing and then making smears on a glass slide with the swab. Under the microscope such cells can often be identified by the pathologist as undeniably malignant. This method is familiar to many women who have undergone the 'cervical smear' test for cancer of the cervix or neck of the womb (see Plate 16). Malignant cells can often be found in the phlegm coughed up by patients with cancer of the lung (see Plate 17) and sometimes in the urine of those with cancer of the bladder. They may be found in the fluid which accumulates around the lung when cancer has spread to invade its surface or in that which forms in the abdomen when cancer spreads through the wall of the bowel. In some cases biopsy can be avoided by puncturing a tumour or an enlarged lymphatic gland with a fine needle, drawing out cells by applying suction with a syringe, and making smears of the contents of the needle on a glass slide. This technique or 'puncture biopsy' can be applied to the liver and the bone marrow and in some centres has been extended to tumours of the lung and the kidney. These methods in which the diagnosis depends upon the study of a few cells or a group of cells demand great experience from the pathologist but they often offer a means of making a firm diagnosis without putting the patient to more than minor discomfort or inconvenience.

It has already been pointed out that most of the blood tests available have only a non-specific value. A positive result indicates that something is amiss but it does not prove that the cause is cancer, nor that any particular organ is the seat of the trouble. For many years hopes have been entertained of finding a blood test which would indicate whether a patient had cancer or not. These hopes have never been fulfilled and it seems most unlikely that they ever will be. There are, however, a few forms of cancer – most of them rare – which do give rise to changes in the blood having some firmer diagnostic value. Some of these are due to the malignant cells making in excess some substance which is the normal product of the organ from which the cancer springs. An example is cancer of the prostate which is often accompanied by an increased quantity in the blood of a substance called acid phosphatase normally made by the cells of the healthy prostate. Another instance is myelomatosis, a cancer of the bone-marrow in which the amount of one of the protein substances of the blood is much increased.

Undoubtedly, more help in the detection and diagnosis of cancer has been given by the X-rays than by any other technological aid. There are many ways in which radiology can be exploited. Simple X-ray photographs have proved indispensable in the diagnosis of cancer of the lung and of the bones. They are being used increasingly in suspected cancer of the breast and the procedure, known as mammography, is discussed more fully in the next chapter on screening. Mammography is of greater value as a screening technique than in one who has already been found to have a tumour in the breast (see Plates 3 and 4).

Many of the more recent developments in radiology depend upon the use of some material, spoken of as a *contrast medium*, opaque to X-rays, which can be used to outline organs which cast no shadow on the film. The most familiar of these techniques is the barium meal in which a patient swallows a 'meal' with which a harmless barium compound has been mixed. The passage of the meal, made opaque by the barium, can be watched on the X-ray screen as it descends the oesophagus and enters the stomach and followed thence on its journey through the intestines. It enables areas of narrowing, ulcers, and tumours which project into the stomach to be outlined and identified. Similarly fluids which are radio-opaque can be injected into the air passages and will show when a bronchus is obstructed, although this method is used less nowadays than it was. The kidneys and particularly the ureters, the ducts carrying urine from the kidneys to the bladder, can be outlined by injecting into a vein a substance which is radio-opaque and excreted in the urine by the kidney. This is indispensable in the diagnosis of cancers of the kidney, urinary passages, and bladder.

Another series of radiological methods entail the injection of a radio-opaque fluid into arteries, veins, or lymphatic vessels. The first and last are of particular value in the diagnosis of cancer. In the first, immediately after the injection a series of radiographs are made rapidly which show up the arrangement of the arteries in the area under investigation. A tumour will greatly alter the normal pattern by displacing arteries and often by leading to the formation of new ones. This method, known as *arteriography*, is used in the identification of tumours of the brain, kidney, and liver (see Plate 9). Injection of contrast-medium into veins is less valuable in this connection although it may sometimes show when the blood flow through a vein is obstructed by a growth.

Cancer – the facts

Radiographs made after the injection of contrast-medium into lymphatic vessels have proved a useful means of identifying enlarged lymphatic glands within the abdomen. In this position they cannot be felt by the examining hand until they have reached a massive size: this radiological technique, known as *lymphangiography or lymphography*, outlines glands even of normal size. Study of the pattern they show on the X-ray film allows a confident opinion on whether they are cancerous or not. It finds its greatest use in the planning of treatment when it is often important to know whether the malignant disease has spread to the glands within the abdomen. This is particularly true of the lymphomas, a group of cancers which arise primarily in the lymphatic glands (see Plate 6).

The most recent development in radiological diagnostic techniques is *'computerized axial tomography'*. This is carried out by an ingenious device which has come to be known as the EMI scanner, for it was developed by Hounsfield working in the EMI research laboratories. The object to be examined is 'scanned' by a succession of pencil-thin X-ray beams emitted by an apparatus which revolves slowly round it. The degree to which that part of the object encountered by each beam impedes the passage of X-rays is measured by a sensitive crystal and recorded by a computer. The process is repeated in a series of 'slices' and all the information assayed by the computer so that the variations in density throughout the entire object can be reproduced photographically. The result is a picture in which tissues of even slightly different 'radio-opacity' stand out in black and white. Originally the method was used only for the head (see Plate 1a). It has proved a revolutionary advance in the detection and localization of brain tumours and capable of distinguishing them from damage due to stroke or other cause. More recently a 'whole body scanner' has been developed. This allows tumours in such inaccessible areas as the pancreas to be precisely outlined as well as showing cancers in the lung, liver, and other internal organs. It requires little imagination to see that this is a method of inestimable value with the added advantage that it

Diagnosis

is a technique of a kind now called 'non-invasive'. The patient suffers no discomfort, no needles are used, and no foreign substances are injected. Moreover it often yields information which cannot be obtained in any other way. The head-scanner has proved its incalculable worth and the whole body scanner is rapidly doing the same (see Plate 18).

Another 'non-invasive' means of investigation which has some value in this field of diagnosis is *ultrasound* or *ultrasonics*. This is founded upon the principle of the Asdic or sonar method used during the last war for detecting submerged submarines. Its worth in cancer is limited, but it can discriminate between solid tumours and cysts which contain fluid. Its chief application is when cancers of the liver, kidney, and ovary are suspected.

The final group of investigative techniques which require mention are those making use of *radioactive isotopes*. Some elements exist in two or more identical chemical forms, spoken of as isotopes of the element. Some isotopes emit radiant activity which others do not. Radioactive isotopes of almost all elements can be produced artificially. The quantity of radiation a radioactive isotope emits gradually decreases, finally ceasing altogether when the isotope reverts to an inactive form of the element. The length of time required for an isotope to lose half its radioactivity is called its 'half-life'.

There are certain chemical substances which have a special affinity for particular tissues in the body. An example is iodine and the thyroid gland. Almost all of a small dose of iodine, whether injected or given by mouth, is concentrated in the thyroid gland before being returned to the blood stream incorporated in thyroid hormone. The amount of radiant activity emitted by an isotope can be measured by a scanner and recorded in photographic form by a special camera. Provided the dose of radioactive isotope is small and its half-life short, such substances can be given without risk. Thus after a dose of radioactive iodine the thyroid gland will become radioactive for a short while and a 'scan' at that time will

51

show whether the radioactivity is regularly distributed throughout its substance. When cancer of the thyroid arises a small tumour can often be felt in the gland; if the scan shows that this nodule does not take up radioactive iodine it has a good chance of being cancerous and should be removed. If it takes up the isotope in the same way as the rest of the gland it is almost certainly benign and can safely be left alone.

The areas of secondary deposits in bones will concentrate the radioactive isotopes of the metals strontium and technetium. A scan of the skeleton will often show metastases as areas of high radioactivity before any change in the bones can be seen on an X-ray film. This may have an important influence on the planning of treatment. Secondary deposits of cancer in the liver will be shown as areas of low radioactivity. Brain tumours can be outlined although here the isotopic scan is likely to be superseded by computerized axial tomography and the same is true of cancer of the pancreas. Isotopic scanning often yields information indispensable for the rational planning of treatment of the patient with cancer.

7

Prevention and 'screening'

The prevention of disease must obviously be the aim of all who are concerned with health and medical care. It is sadly true that the traditional training of doctors encourages them to think entirely in terms of treating established disease; while the public, or large sections of it, prefers to dismiss all thoughts of illness from its mind until circumstances make its recognition inescapable. Consequently all preventive measures have two obstacles to surmount and in the case of cancer the second is particularly significant. Nevertheless, there are a number of ways in which some forms of cancer can be prevented or at least made less common: many of these can be deduced from the discussion of the known causes in an earlier chapter.

There are a few rare cancers in which heredity plays an important part. When there is an appreciable risk of their offspring displaying one of these, a married couple might be thought to have a duty to consider whether parenthood was justifiable. Family planning organizations are prepared to explain the severity of the risk and the potential parents must then decide whether it is acceptable. Fortunately, cancers of this type are rare: the commonest, the *retinoblastoma*, is a tumour which arises from the retina at the back of the eye. It occurs in 20 000 births: thus in England and Wales some thirty babies are born each year who will develop this cancer. In only 1 in 10 of these is another member of the family affected. In two-thirds of the babies tumours appear in each eye. Of the offspring of those who have survived and become capable of parenthood, but where no other member of the family is affected, 10–20 per cent will develop retinoblastoma when one eye of the parent has been diseased and 50 per cent when both eyes were affected.

Another disorder with a hereditary basis is *polyposis of the colon*, in which numerous fleshy wart-like growths develop from the lining membrane of the large bowel. In three-quarters of those with polyposis of the colon other members of the family are affected and simple transmission from parent to child is the rule. When they appear the polyps are benign, but eventually one or more becomes undeniably malignant and it is generally accepted that the entire colon should be removed to avoid the otherwise certain development of cancer.

It is recognized that mongols are more likely to develop cancer than normal children. The particular form of malignant disease to which they are laible is acute leukaemia and the risk of their developing this is fifteen times greater than that of a normal child. *Mongolism* can be diagnosed early in pregnancy by examining cells in the 'water' in the mother's womb. It has been suggested that when the risk is high, this test should be carried out and the pregnancy terminated if it shows that the child is likely to be a mongol.

There is a growing belief that many cancers are caused by carcinogens in the environment, a term expanded to include the contents of the stomach and bowels. Every year many thousand new chemical compounds are synthesized and used in industry, agriculture, and scientific laboratories. It is unknown and difficult to determine which are likely to be carcinogenic. It may take years of exposure to a chemical substance before it becomes clear that it is a cause of cancer. If it induces malignant change in animals it may not do so in man, although no substance known to be carcinogenic in man has yet failed to cause cancer in the experimental animal. Attempts are continuously being made to devise tests of carcinogenicity which are reliable and rapid, but as yet they have not been successful. The only dependable test is the retrospective one and by the time this can be applied the damage has been done.

At present it is impossible to foretell whether the environment in an industrial plant contains carcinogens which have not yet been identified and only general precautionary measures such as cleanliness at work, control of dust, adequate ventilation, and protective clothing can be applied. When tests on animals prove a substance to be carcinogenic, it is usually withdrawn from the market although anomalies may arise. An example is the sweetener, cyclamate, which was found to cause cancer of the bladder in rats. The daily dose required to achieve this result would in man be equivalent to the quantity contained in several thousand bottles of sweetened mineral water.

There are, on the other hand, a number of well-recognized carcinogens which may be encountered in the environment. The most important, for they can be most easily controlled, are those concerned with occupations. Pott's chimney sweeps' cancer has already been mentioned. The bladder cancer of workers in the dye and rubber industries, the lung cancer due to exposure to asbestos, nickel, and chromium, and the nasal cancer of furniture workers are further examples. The presence of carcinogens in all these instances is appreciated and precautions against them can be taken. Radioactivity is another risk in certain occupations, such as uranium and pitchblende miners, radiologists, and workers in nuclear plants. Here again protection is possible and can be imposed by authority upon those liable to exposure.

In the social environment other carcinogens are recognizable. These cannot be controlled by a beneficient authority and require the co-operation of the individual. The most important of these is cigarette smoke and the part it plays in the cause of cancer of the lung is familiar to all. It is also of some importance in other cancers, particularly those of the nasal passages, mouth, throat, and oesophagus. It has been held, on less secure evidence, to be a factor in the cause of cancers of the bladder and the pancreas. The virtually complete failure of publicity campaigns to alter the smoking habits of the nation and particularly of the young shows how difficult it is to control carcinogens when voluntary effort and self-denial are required. Indeed, the only group in society in which the proportion of smokers has notably decreased and lung cancer become less common is the medical profession. Understandably its members have a better insight than most into the ravages of lung cancer.

There are certain malignant diseases which statistics show to be associated with heavy drinking. Predictably these are cancers of the oesophagus and stomach. Indirectly primary cancer of the liver falls into this group because, although rare in this country, it almost always arises in a liver affected by cirrhosis which may be the result of prolonged alcohol excess. Heavy drinking is so often associated with heavy smoking that it is difficult in some instances to know how much responsibility to attach to each.

In a different category is cancer of the cervix or neck of the womb. There is good evidence that this tumour is more common in the promiscuous and in those women whose sexual activity starts in early youth. One writer has described it as an 'occupational disease of prostitutes'. It has been known for many years to be rare in nuns. There have been suggestions that the contraceptive pill might be a factor in the cause of cancer of the cervix, but this has been proved untrue. Nevertheless the contraceptive pill has removed the traditional penalty for promiscuity and thus makes an indirect contribution.

Many workers are suspicious that the diet contains carcinogens as yet unidentified. The possibility of aflatoxin being responsible for the frequency of primary cancer of the liver in the Bantu and some other nations of Africa and Asia is noted in Chapter 2; so too is the suggestion that cancer of the large bowel is related to constipation and exposure to carcinogens which the intestinal bacteria synthesize from bile. Neither of these hypotheses has been proven; indeed proof would demand the demonstration that complete control of the suspected substance was followed by a significant decrease in the incidence of the cancer for which it was blamed. Nevertheless suspicion is sufficient to make it worth ensuring that meal is stored hygienically and that the bowel habit is regularized.

Prevention and 'screening'

A final group of known carcinogens are medicinal. The relationship between cancer of the vagina in teenaged girls and treatment of their mothers in pregnancy with diethylstilboestrol to prevent miscarriage is well recognized. Happily incidents of this kind are excessively rare, and until recently the possible sequence was quite unsuspected. Prolonged treatment of menopausal symptoms with oestrogen, another female hormone, is believed to increase the risk of developing cancer of the body of the womb. In the past prolonged medication with arsenic has caused skin cancer. Some of the newer drugs used in the treatment of malignant disease may predispose to the appearance of other types of cancer. A number of patients with myelomatosis, a neoplasm of the bone-marrow, have, after responding well to chemotherapy, developed acute leukaemia. It is possible that this is the result of the drug used in treatment impairing the body's immunity mechanism. Support is given to this by the experience with patients who have received kidney transplants. A kidney graft is regarded by the tissues of its recipient as 'foreign' in the same fashion as invading bacteria are, and the body's protective potential is mobilized in an attempt to destroy it. This 'immune response' can lead to death and rejection of the graft unless it is suppressed by various drugs. Experience of the past few years has shown that patients who have received grafts and are taking what are called 'immuno-suppressive' drugs have an increased liability to primary cancers: such tumours are often of bizarre type.

In another category are drugs which cause cancer by their irritant properties. An example is cyclophosphamide which is widely used in the treatment of malignant disease. After being taken by mouth or injected it undergoes changes in the body and part is filtered off by the kidney and passed into the urine. This waste product may cause irritation of the bladder, leading to inflammation and, in one or two cases, cancer has developed. It is easily avoided by making certain that large amounts of water are drunk while the drug is being taken so that the irritant in the urine is diluted. This unhappy sequel was always rare, and never occurs now that smaller doses are given and this simple precaution observed.

A final group of preventive measures concerns the recognition and treatment of precancerous states. It has been explained in an earlier chapter that there are a number of circumstances in which there is a high risk of cancer developing. Polyps of the colon are liable to become malignant and should be removed. In multiple polyposis of the colon, mentioned earlier, complete removal of the large bowel is required for cancerous change is certain. There is a greatly increased risk of cancer of the large bowel in ulcerative colitis and this danger grows with the passage of years. Removal of the colon is recommended more and more frequently. Benign tumours of the urinary bladder frequently become malignant and are always removed or destroyed. Cancer of the penis, a rare disease, has never been seen in those circumcised in infancy and this is used as an argument in favour of this operation.

Sometimes changes occur in the mucous membrane of the mouth and elsewhere causing thickened white plaques and known as leukoplakia. This is a recognized precancerous state and may require preventive surgery. Precancerous changes in the skin and on the cervix of the womb are not uncommon and are discussed in the following paragraphs.

The expressions 'screening' or 'health screening' have come to mean the routine examination of apparently healthy people at regular intervals with a view to discovering signs of disease before symptoms arise. Its rationale is the assumption that all disease is more easily cured or arrested the earlier treatment is started. The notion sprang from the results of examining large number of young men prior to their joining the Armed Forces at the outbreak of the Boer War and later of the First World War. The authorities were alarmed to find the low general standard of health in these recruits, but it was only after the Second World War that regular medical examinations became an accepted practice. At first these were preliminary to appointments in order to protect the interests

58

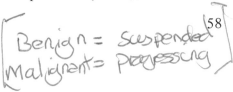

Benign = suspended
Malignant = progressing

of employers. Now, particularly in the United States, the routine 'check-up' has become part of the standard medical care expected by the middle-class executive. The practice is gradually spreading in this country.

The value of such regular examinations has been accepted as self-evident. It is only recently that it has been questioned. It is difficult to devise a method of measuring any benefit that screening may confer, but a careful comparison over the years of two similar groups of persons, one screened regularly and the other not at all, has shown no difference in the length of survival between the two. From this, using the length of survival as the only yardstick, the investigator concluded that there was no evidence that screening was of any advantage to anyone. In spite of this conclusion there may well be more subtle benefits; for it improves morale and, although it may generate anxiety in a few, it relieves unfounded worries in many.

These comments refer to general health screening and not to screening specifically for cancer. Screening for cancer can reasonably be condemned because of the impossibility of proving a negative. There is never an occasion on which a doctor has scientific justification for telling a patient that he has not got cancer. A moment's reflection will show the truth of this statement. Cancer in its earliest stages is only with difficulty identified, and then only when the tissue can be studied under the microscope. It is clear that it will have to advance considerably before it can be detected by the relatively gross methods we have for examining the human body. Moreover routine screening for cancer would demand not only physical examination but radiological, cytological, isotopic and endoscopic investigations of the lungs, stomach, bowels, kidneys, bladder, liver, bones, nose, and throat. Whatever criteria are used, this exercise could not be described as cost-effective and it is probable that the considerable X-ray dosage required might cause more cancer than it detected.

Nevertheless there are valid arguments for screening for specific cancers. It is generally accepted that the earlier

Cancer – the facts

treatment for malignant disease is started, the better the outlook. This is probably true of the many forms of cancer which are curable and it is therefore logical to make all reasonable efforts to detect them in as early a stage as possible. In this respect a greater understanding of the problems of cancer by the public is essential. It is sometimes argued by the medical profession that 'cancer education' does no more than foster an ineradicable anxiety in the lay mind. There are some of whom this may be true, but the majority are intelligent rational beings who are as capable of holding balanced views as the doctors. It is important that the mystique which surrounds malignant disease be dispelled. Only when this has been done will the patient with cancer be able to face the facts of his illness with equanimity and understanding and make an essential contribution to his care by informed co-operation.

The simplest form of screening might be called 'self-examination'. Undoubtedly an awareness of the possibility of cancer should exist, but it must be prevented from degenerating into an obsessional preoccupation with the problem. The American Cancer Society has described what it calls the 'Seven Warning Signals', the appearance of any one of which should lead to early consultation with the doctor. They are as follows:

1. A change in bowel or bladder habit.
2. A sore or ulcer which does not heal.
3. Unusual bleeding or discharge.
4. A thickening or lump in the breast or elsewhere.
5. Indigestion or difficulty in swallowing.
6. Obvious change in a wart or mole.
7. An irritating cough or hoarseness.

In addition to reporting such symptoms or abnormalities to the doctor, members of the public are often advised to examine themselves regularly. Clearly this cannot be more than superficial. It can include the body surface and women have been urged to examine their breasts meticulously and to report the findings of any thickening, discharge from the nipple, puckering of the skin or lump. It has been suggested too that specimens of the motions should be sent to the laboratory at regular intervals to be tested for the presence of blood. If the tests prove positive examinations will be necessary to make certain that the bleeding is not due to a cancer of the stomach or intestine.

Two common varieties of cancer are those of the female breast and the neck of the womb, and screening to exclude the presence of malignant disease in these areas has become a standard practice. Mention of the 'cervical smear' test has already been made. It is estimated that about 2 000 000 of these tests are now made each year in England and Wales. The method is simple and often carried out by a nurse. The neck of the womb is inspected for any abnormality; a swab is taken from the mucous membrane and smeared onto a microscope slide where it leaves a film of cells. The slides are examined under the microscope by a pathologist who will be able to classify the cells as either normal; abnormal but not clearly malignant; or definitely malignant (see Plate 16). In the third case a cone of tissue is removed by the surgeon and further microscopic examination will show whether the malignant cells have begun to invade the surrounding normal tissue (invasive carcinoma) or whether the change is a purely local one (carcinoma-in-situ). In this second case the cone biopsy is curative, removing all the cancerous cells. If the tests show invasive carcinoma a more extensive operation is required. When the cells in the smear are abnormal but not clearly malignant they are described as 'dysplastic' and regular cervical smears are made at intervals which vary from three to six months depending upon the degree of dysplasia. When the smears show only normal cells, routine yearly tests should continue.

There are several points which are still uncertain. It is not known whether every example of carcinoma-in-situ inevitably progresses to the stage of invasive cancer. It appears that the first is much more common than would have been expected from the total number of patients with overt cancer of the cervix. Thus it is likely that some cases of carcinoma-in-situ advance no further and recover spontaneously. It is possible that dysplasia can advance without a detectable stage of carcinoma-in-situ to true invasive cancer. Some gynaecologists believe that if a woman is over 35 years old and has no more reproductive ambitions it is wise to undertake radical operation and remove the entire womb in all those with dysplasia or carcinoma-in-situ.

Like many methods which are preventive rather than curative, it is difficult to prove that the wide use of the cervical smear test has had a beneficial effect. Cancer of the cervix is predominantly a disease of women in the lower income groups. They are much less easy than their well-to-do sisters to convince that the test is worthwhile. Nevertheless in Aberdeen over some 10 years more than 97 per cent of married women below the age of 60 years have been examined by the cervical smear method and, by acting upon the findings, the numbers consulting the doctor with cancer of the cervix have been reduced by one-third. In British Columbia the test has been almost universally applied for the last 20 years. Over this period there has been a steady decrease in the numbers in Canada certified as dying from this form of cancer, but the death rate in women aged 45–60 years has fallen more rapidly in British Columbia than elsewhere in the Dominion.

Carcinoma of the breast is the commonest variety of cancer in women. It remains a disease which presents many unsolved problems and it is distressing that the outlook now should be little better than it was 50 years ago. It is however fairly established that when the disease is completely confined to the breast, the chances of complete and permanent cure are far greater than if it has spread even only to the lymphatic glands in its vicinity. It is reasonable to assume that the 'earlier' the diagnosis is made, the more likely is the disease to be a purely local one. It is worth repeating that the term 'early' is often used when speaking of cancer, but does not bear close examination. It means little more than when the tumour first becomes detectable. It is unknown how rapidly the tumour grows, indeed different cancers grow at widely different rates. One may perhaps be detectable three months after the first changes of malignancy appear in the cells, while another may have taken as many years to reach the same size. Notwithstanding, it is generally accepted that identification of a cancer of the breast as soon as it can be detected and its immediate treatment are the only practicable ways of improving the outlook.

Physical examination is naturally the first step. The patient herself may indeed have noticed a swelling in the breast, but if the examination is part of the screening programme, it is undertaken by a doctor or nurse. It has been proved that, after a short training, nurses are as competent as doctors in detecting any abnormalities in the breast. Within recent years there have been several technical advances in the diagnosis of this disease. The first is X-ray examination. It is spoken of as mammography and consists of taking an X-ray photograph of the breast using an especially sensitive film. The fine details of the breast's structure can be seen because the translucent fat provides an excellent contrast. Benign breast tumours which are common show as sharply outlined shadows with clear-cut margins. The edges of the shadow thrown by a cancer are indefinite and irregular projections into the surrounding breast tissue can be seen (see Plate 5).

A refinement of mammography has recently been introduced. It is known as xerography and differs from it in that a selenium plate is substituted for the normal radiographic film. It gives a sharper definition of abnormal shadows in the breast.

A third technique is thermography. It was noted many years ago that the skin overlying a cancer of the breast often felt warm. Precise temperature recordings of the skin gave significantly higher readings over the tumour and a photographic record can be made with the warmer areas dark and the cooler pale. Thermography has proved a useful supplement to mammography.

Cancer – the facts

The difficulties discussed earlier apply with equal force to assessing the benefits of screening for cancer of the breast. Convincing evidence would be provided only by including all women in a defined geographical area and of a given age group. In every published report some women have attended for screening in response to invitation, some because of symptoms or anxiety, and some have been referred by their doctors.

One of the earliest studies came from New York. Only women aged 50 years or over were invited to attend and 1 in every 200 (0.4 per cent) without symptoms was found to have cancer of the breast. Physical examination revealed 44 per cent of the cancers and one-third were detected by mammography. The claim is made that this screening procedure has reduced by one-third the deaths from this disease in women over the age of 50 years.

In several large practices in Edinburgh all women between the ages of 40 and 50 years were invited to attend for screening. 3952, or 81.8 per cent of those invited responded; 5.4 per cent of these were considered to require further investigation and 18, or 0.46 per cent proved to have cancer. Of these 6 were women aged between 40 and 50 years. The cost of each screening was estimated at £16.50 and the discovery of each cancer at £6000.

In a Swedish study 37 640 were examined by mammography only and cancer was found in 125, or 0.33 per cent. In Holland more than 14 000 women aged 50–64 years were examined clinically and by mammography, 106 were found to have cancer; but only one was discovered by clinical examination.

In a Manchester series three groups of women were screened for cancer of the breast. The first consisted of 1671 over the age of 50 years, being 54 per cent responding to an invitation to attend the centre; the second was of 1055 attending spontaneously and uninvited; and the third of 1945 referred by their doctors because of suspected breast disease. The incidence of cancer in the three groups was 0.96 per cent, 0.66 per cent, and 9.15 per cent respectively. Cancers were found in 15 women completely free from symptoms, an incidence of 0.73 per cent.

Prevention and 'screening'

These series show that between 4 and 8 women in every 1000 over the age of 40 years and without symptoms are found by screening to have cancer of the breast. It is probable that not more than half of these can be detected without mammography. The smaller the cancer when treatment is undertaken the better the outlook. These considerations leave no doubt that routine screening for breast cancer in women over the age of 40 years is worthwhile.

The wisdom of exposing the breast to the irradiation required for mammography has often been questioned. With the sensitive films in use and other refinements of technique the dose of irradiation has been reduced to a level which all would regard as insignificant. It has been estimated that the dose used would induce 6 new cases of breast cancer per 1 000 000 per year after an interval of 10 years. Thus there is no appreciable risk after the age of 50 years. It is true that in young women in whom there is less fat and more glandular tissue in the breast a somewhat higher dose is required. It has been recommended that in them the use of mammography should be restricted to diagnosis and that screening of the apparently healthy should be avoided.

Other forms of cancer which could be detected before the appearance of symptoms are many, but in most screening is impracticable. Lung cancer, because of its frequency, has a particular importance. X-ray examination of the lungs is a routine measure in all screening programmes and unsuspected cancer is not a rare discovery. Further tests are required to establish the diagnosis beyond doubt and they include examination of the phlegm to see whether it contains cancer cells, and perhaps bronchoscopy (see Chapter 6). It remains uncertain how much benefit results. Removal of the lung, or of a lobe of the lung containing the cancer at the present time offers the only hope of cure. In not more than one patient in five do the conditions justify even attempting operation. Nevertheless until some more effective treatment is available and while cigarette smoking continues at its present level the 'early' detection and treatment of lung cancer is important.

Cancer – the facts

Screening can, of course, detect cancer in areas open to direct inspection such as the skin surface, the tongue, and the mouth. These are regions in which the individual can scarcely fail to note the signs of disease although he may postpone reporting them to his doctor. Indeed this failure to seek advice at once is a major cause for concern and one of the problems which only education of the public will solve.

Three-quarters of all cancers of the large bowel occur within range of the sigmoidoscope, an instrument which can be passed easily and painlessly into its lower reaches. It has been suggested that this examination should form part of the routine screening programme. In one report from the United States of 40 000 such examinations in persons over 40 years of age and without bowel symptoms 0.13 per cent were found to have cancer. Thus 10 000 routine sigmoidoscopic examinations were required to discover one cancer. The average age of those affected was 67 years and the estimated cost of prolonging one life by perhaps 3 or 4 years was between $100 000 and $200 000.

In Japan where cancer of the stomach has a higher incidence than anywhere else in the world screening has been developed in some centres in an attempt to achieve earlier diagnosis. In Osaka 260 cancers were found in 78 404 patients submitted to gastroscopy, an incidence of 0.33 per cent. Of these 1 in 3 were early and localized compared with the usual finding of 1 in 20.

Screening in general as well as for cancer is only in its infancy in this country, but any further developments should be examined critically. It is a costly process in medical and paramedical manpower, in buildings and in equipment. Although it has come to be regarded *a priori* as a beneficient activity, there is little solid evidence that anyone derives any advantage from it, although screening for cancer of the breast and of the cervix are probable exceptions. In the present climate of economic famine, critical appraisal of the benefits likely to flow from any screening programme is advisable before commitment is made.

8

Treatment

The cure of cancer is seldom complete within a day or two and, indeed, the sad but familiar truth is that cure is sometimes not to be anticipated. Whatever the outlook it is likely that the sufferer will be under the doctor's care for a matter of weeks or months. Consequently from his point of view the selection of his doctor is one of the more important therapeutic considerations. Chance and availability often determine his choice, but clearly the ideal doctor should be one the patient believes to be competent and in whom he can put his trust, but he must also be one he finds agreeable and in whom he feels he can confide. On the other hand, it is unwise for both doctor and patient to allow a satisfactory professional relationship to acquire a social quality. It has been said 'Never make a friend of your doctor, nor your doctor of a friend'. If this austere precept is not observed, the doctor cannot but become emotionally entangled, his detachment will be lost and his judgement impaired.

The adequate care of a patient with cancer will often require the co-operation and advice of a number of experts: the surgeon, the radiotherapist, and that newest of all, the oncologist or cancer specialist, may all be needed. Although this is inevitable there are disadvantages in being under the care of a committee and these can only be offset by a strong chairman who is capable of weighing the advice and taking responsibility for the decisions. Treatment by consensus leads to fumbling indecision and often ends in catastrophe.

The aim of treatment of the sufferer from cancer must always be complete and enduring cure. Although in a high proportion of cases this can confidently be anticipated, there are only too many occasions when it is manifestly impossible and no more than palliation can be achieved. Three therapeutic weapons are available: surgery, radiotherapy, and chemotherapy. Surgery needs no definition. Radiotherapy is treatment by exposure to ionizing rays such as those emitted by an X-ray tube. Chemotherapy is treatment by chemical substances, either naturally occurring or man-made – that is, treatment by drugs. Two other methods deserve comment. The first is treatment with hormones which are the natural products of the body's internal or endocrine glands. This is capable in some cancers of leading to prolonged, but never permanent, relief. The second is immunological and attempts to mobilize the body's own defence against the cancer. This method has proved bitterly disappointing and has so far provided no practical benefit.

Every sufferer from cancer presents an individual problem. Although there are well-defined standard methods of treatment they cannot be applied by rule of thumb. First the exact nature of the cancer must be established and this may require a biopsy as discussed in Chapter 6. It is a cardinal rule that whenever possible the diagnosis must be confirmed by a microscopic study of material from the tumour. Secondly, the exact extent of the cancer must be determined. The primary tumour must be delineated and the presence or absence of spread to lymphatic glands as well as of distant blood-borne metastases determined. Thirdly, the general health of the patient must be considered, other disabilities such as heart disease, diabetes, or chronic bronchitis must be excluded or identified and treated, and his psychological as well as his physical stamina assessed. It is only when all this information is available that a rational scheme of treatment can be planned. But this does not end the problems of management for the support needed to maintain general health and morale is almost as important as radical curative treatment.

Surgery still holds pride of place. That it should do is an admission of failure, for every operation which entails excision of a part of the body, even when a technical *tour de force*, is a mutilation. Nevertheless in many types of cancer it

Treatment

offers the best, and often the only, chance of cure. The decision to advise surgery depends upon two considerations: first, that the proposed operation is technically possible, and secondly that there are no distant metastases. It is for this second reason that careful review of the extent of the disease is essential before the decision is reached. A final factor which may reasonably exert an influence is an appraisal of the natural history and aggressive qualities of the type of cancer in question as judged by microscopic study of the tumour and past experience of similar cases.

Even when all the portents are favourable there are other points to be considered. First, it is clear that surgery cannot be justified when the number dying as a result of the operation is unduly high. It is not easy to define the phrase 'unduly high'. In many instances operation offers the only chance of cure and the alternative is a painful and disabling illness inevitably ending in death. It may well be in the patient's best interests for the risk to be accepted. In this decision his physical and psychological resources are of paramount importance. It is reasonable to enquire who should make the decision and the answer to this question quite clearly must be the patient. He should make it in the light of a frank and honest assessment of the position by his doctor. The second point is to decide whether the mutilation resulting from the operation is acceptable. It is not only the aesthetic consequences which have to be considered, indeed, these are seldom of overriding importance when it is a matter of life or death. The functional effects can be disastrous. An example would be the removal of a lung in cancer from a chronic bronchitic, when operation may result in shortness of breath severe enough to make life insupportable. Finally, if cure or results comparable to those of surgery can be attained by any other means, operation is almost always advisable.

In the preceding paragraphs the general points which would influence a decision in favour of radical curative surgery have been discussed. Even when cure is impossible operation may have an important palliative role. Removal of a large tumour

69

may do much to lessen discomfort or pain. Surgery is often justifiable for the relief of obstruction of the bowel or of the bile duct. There are some cancers which depend upon the secretion of hormones from various endocrine glands. When the secretion is abolished by excision of the gland producing it, the growth of the cancer may be arrested. Examples are the effects of removal of the ovaries, the suprarenal glands, or the pituitary gland in some cases of cancer of the breast, and of castration in cancer of the prostate.

Finally, there are two unusual situations in which surgery may be required. The first is when a solitary metastasis makes its appearance some years after the primary cancer has been removed. Provided there is virtual certainty that there are no other secondary deposits and that there has been no recurrence of the primary cancer, removal of the metastasis may be justifiable if it is feasible. This situation arises, perhaps, most often when the primary tumour is in the kidney where excision of a solitary metastasis has often been curative. The second problem is more common. In this case an obvious metastasis is found, but exhaustive investigation fails to reveal the site of the primary cancer. Often this is a single enlarged lymphatic gland in one of the groups on the surface of the body, perhaps in the neck or groin. The diagnosis is confirmed by removing the gland and by its examination by the pathologist. This is often followed by radiotherapy to the area from which it was excised. Sometimes the symptoms of a brain tumour appear and needle biopsy shows it to be a secondary deposit. This sequence is most common with primary cancer of the lung, but at times meticulous search reveals no primary growth. The decision of whether to remove the tumour or not is often a difficult one.

The second mainstay of cancer treatment, radiotherapy, has been in use since the early years of this century. It consists of exposing the tumour and its immediate neighbourhood to rays emitted by an X-ray tube, radium, a radioactive isotope of cobalt or caesium, or by other devices such as the linear accelerator or the cyclotron. This ionizing radiation is capable

Treatment

of killing both normal and malignant cells. It exerts its lethal effect when the cell is in the process of dividing; thus, those cells which divide rapidly and frequently are most sensitive to its action. In general cancer cells divide more frequently than healthy cells, although those in the bone-marrow which make the cells of the blood and those which line the stomach and bowel are an exception. The difference in sensitivity between malignant and healthy cells is almost entirely dictated by the frequency of their division, thus radiotherapy has no special selective effect upon cancer cells and is almost always associated with some damage to healthy tissue. Healthy cells, however, recover more rapidly and more completely than malignant cells from injury which falls short of being lethal. Thus if repeated doses of radiation are given with intervals between, the intermissions will give the healthy cells time to repair the damage while the next dose will be sufficient to kill many of the cancer cells which have not recovered from the previous injury.

The amount of radiation is measured in units called rads and treatment is usually given as a series of daily doses in order to take advantage of the capacity of healthy tissue to recover. Usually four or five treatments are given each week. Dividing the dose into small fractions in this fashion means that the total quantity of irradiation needed to achieve a given effect will be much greater than if a single dose were used. Thus a single dose of 2200 rads has the same effect as one of 5200 rads given as fifteen equal doses spread over 21 days. The single dose, however, would cause unacceptable damage to normal tissue in the area treated.

Some cancers are sensitive to radiotherapy while others are almost entirely resistant. Those that can be cured are few and the accumulated experience of 75 years has given radiotherapists precise knowledge of what they are able to achieve. Cancer of the testicle is one of the most sensitive and cure by radiotherapy is often possible even when there are extensive metastases. Some varieties of cancer of the cervix are now usually treated in this way and so too are some brain tumours.

71

It can also cure Hodgkin's disease in its early stages.

Radiotherapy is sometimes used in combination with surgery. It may be possible by irradiating a cancer which cannot be removed surgically to shrink it to a size where operation is possible. It is also used after operation, particularly when the surgeon is uncertain whether he has removed the whole tumour, but also in the hope of destroying any undetected spread of the growth.

Radiotherapy has a valuable part to play in palliative treatment when it is prescribed with a view to the relief of symptoms and not with the aim of cure. It can shrink tumours and thus relieve pain and symptoms due to pressure. Examples are its use in reducing the size of a tumour within the chest which interferes with breathing or of one pressing on the spinal cord leading to paralysis of the legs. The often intense pain due to secondary malignant deposits in bones can usually be abolished by radiotherapy. It must be admitted, however, that this form of treatment has often been used in circumstances where cure is impossible and relief of symptoms improbable. It can readily be understood how distressing a doctor finds it to tell a patient, aware that surgery and radiotherapy are the only available forms of treatment, that he is unlikely to benefit from either. The temptation to advise a short course of radiotherapy 'for psychological reasons' is an attractive although cowardly alternative. This questionable role is now more often allotted to chemotherapy.

Radiotherapy can give rise to reactions which make the recipient seriously ill although such an event is exceptional nowadays. It is the sensitive cells which form the blood and those which line the stomach and intestines which bear the brunt of the damage. Radiation sickness is especially liable to occur when the abdomen has to be included in the area treated. It shows itself by nausea, vomiting, a distaste for food, abdominal discomfort and diarrhoea. It never lasts for more than 48 hours after the course of treatment is finished, thus if symptoms continue longer, another cause for them must be sought. The effect of radiation on the blood-forming

72

u didn't look at what the facts/truth is ~ u only saw what u wanted 2 c ie. cure.

cells is shown by a fall in the number of white blood cells in the circulation. Since these are one of the body's main defences against microbes, a profound drop in their number will open the door to severe infection. To prevent such complications regular examinations of the blood are made on all patients undergoing radiotherapy. In addition to these well-defined disturbances there is often complaint of overwhelming lassitude and disinclination for all mental and physical effort, particularly when large areas are being treated.

The other untoward effects of irradiation are the result of local damage in the area treated. The skin is sensitive and will often become intensely red and sore, after larger doses it may become paper-thin and over its surface show minute but distended blood vessels. When a brain tumour has to be treated, there is inevitably temporary loss of hair in the area irradiated. In the great majority the hair grows again and often returns to normal, but the extent and duration of the damage depends upon the dose of irradiation. If the mouth or throat is included in the field of treatment, the secretions are temporarily abolished and there is uncomfortable dryness. Exposure of either the ovaries or the testicles to irradiation can lead to sterility. The first may occur when abdominal treatment is required, although methods of shielding them have been devised. The testicles are more easily protected and thus are rarely damaged.

The third member of this therapeutic triad is chemotherapy. In this context it may be defined as the treatment of cancer by chemical agents or drugs. It is perhaps illogical not to include under this head treatment by hormones, but it has become the convention to separate the two. For centuries a medicinal cure for cancer has been sought and as long ago as 1865 a German surgeon, Billroth, found that arsenic was of value in the treatment of some malignant diseases.

The story of chemotherapy over the last 40 years provides an illuminating demonstration that science does not always advance by orderly and logical steps. During the Second World War research into the effects of mustard gas showed that in animals it led to a great reduction in the number of white blood cells in the circulation. It was suggested that this property might make it useful in the treatment of leukaemia, a disease in which the number of white blood cells is commonly much increased. It proved, indeed, to be of considerable, although temporary, benefit and trials of it and of similar chemical compounds were extended to the treatment of patients with Hodgkin's disease, a form of cancer related to leukaemia. It was even more effective and this observation became the starting point of an all-embracing search for drugs which might prove efficacious in the treatment of cancer. Many other chemical compounds related to mustard gas were tried in addition to a vast number of synthetic and naturally occurring substances. Indeed, in the 20 years following the discovery of the anticancer properties of mustard gas some 90 000 different compounds were tested for similar effects. This immense effort reaped but a paltry harvest, for at the end only fifteen to twenty drugs of therapeutic value emerged.

When chemotherapy for cancer was first introduced it was used with the tacit, and often unconscious, assumption that it was not going to achieve cure and that, even if there was immediate benefit, relapse was inevitable. Thus the drugs were administered in low doses given continuously until relapse did occur when a change was made to another drug in the hope of attaining a further remission. Gradually methods changed. First intermittent treatment with a larger dose was used, then combinations of drugs were prescribed. All anticancer drugs are poisonous when given in excess, but different substances often cause different ill-effects. It was argued that if two or more drugs active against cancer, but causing different ill-effects, were used doses of each just insufficient to lead to poisoning could be given simultaneously without upsetting the patient. This combination would, it was hoped, increase the anticancer effect some two- or three-fold. At the present time cancer chemotherapy usually takes this pattern: combinations of drugs are given in high doses separated by intervals in which healthy cells can recover from the earlier onslaught. The action of all antineoplastic drugs is similar to that of radiotherapy for in both the cell is most vulnerable at the time of division, although the ways in which the two methods inflict their damage differ.

Chemotherapy is capable of curing few forms of cancer. It is justifiable to claim that it can be completely effective in some cases of Hodgkin's disease, acute leukaemia, a rare kidney cancer in children (nephroblastoma), an equally rare cancer of muscles (rhabdomyosarcoma), and an even rarer cancer of the placenta ('afterbirth'), called choriocarcinoma. Different drugs are required for different cancers and the programmes for treatment and the intervals between doses and between courses vary widely. Indeed, it is true to say that chemotherapy is developing so rapidly and that new drugs make their appearance so frequently that programmes of treatment recommended one month may be outdated a few weeks later.

Chemotherapy is an important adjuvant form of treatment. It has been used during surgery because the manipulation inevitable at operation has been suspected of setting free cancer cells and causing metastases. It has been used after operation for the same reason. It has been combined with radiotherapy. It has been recommended after removal of a mass of tumour even when surgical cure is not regarded as possible. In this case it is argued that, if as much of the cancer as possible is removed, the antineoplastic drug is likely to be more effective for there will be fewer cells for it to attack.

The place of chemotherapy in palliative treatment has already been mentioned. There are circumstances even when the disease is far advanced and there are many metastases in which it may bring temporary benefit. Particularly in patients with disseminated cancer of the breast and extensive cancer of the ovary chemotherapy may temporarily obliterate all evidence of disease and allow a period of relatively normal life.

It is always difficult to be certain that no improvement can be expected. There is a tendency therefore to make use of it when even transient remission is most improbable. It must never be forgotten that this treatment often makes its recipient feel desperately ill and that these powerful drugs are poisons which can damage the general health. It is not always humane to burden a dying man with this additional and probably unrewarding load.

Some forms of malignant disease can be checked, albeit temporarily, by treatment with hormones. The notion that the glands of internal secretion, the endocrine glands, might have an influence on the growth of cancer is of long-standing. It dates from Beatson of Glasgow who showed in 1896 that removal of the ovaries greatly benefitted women with advanced cancer of the breast. In 1941 Huggins, a Chicago surgeon, found that men with cancer of the prostate were improved by castration. Regarding the male and female sex hormones as in some ways mutually antagonistic, the next logical step was to see whether male hormones improved women with cancer of the breast and female, men with cancer of the prostate. In both cases this proved to be so. At least one-quarter of women with advanced cancer of the breast before the change of life improve greatly when given an androgen or male sex hormone. Removal of the ovaries will help one-half. After the menopause the position is different: perhaps one-fifth of women derive benefit from an oestrogen, a female sex hormone, and a similar proportion from removal of the suprarenal glands or even the pituitary gland. The explanation is not clear. The response of the man with prostatic cancer is even more dramatic. Between 80 and 85 per cent are relieved of all symptoms and all signs of the disease vanish. This is remission, but not cure; nevertheless it may endure for 5 or even 10 years. Symptoms finally return and the growth resists further treatment with hormones.

Progesterone – another female sex hormone – has proved useful in treating cancer of the body of the womb. It causes remission in about one-third of elderly women with advanced malignant disease of this type. It has also been recommended in cancer of the kidney, although here its effects are debatable. The cortisone group of hormones — the corticosteroids — have been widely used in the treatment of cancer. Many are, of course, synthetic and are thus not strictly hormones although they have effects similar to the prototype hormone, cortisone. They are effective in combination with other drugs in the treatment of acute leukaemia of children where a remission rate of 90 per cent can be achieved and, there is every reason to believe, cure is attainable. In advanced cancer of the breast they are also of value: one-fifth of those with advanced disease will report improvement, although in only half of these will the signs of disease regress. The corticosteroids are often used in patients with advanced or terminal cancer for their 'tonic' properties. They may relieve depression and stimulate appetite, but have no more specific effect.

The various methods of treatment described are often used in combination. The ways in which they can complement each other have already been mentioned. Radiotherapy can be used before or after surgery. Chemotherapy may be prescribed after operation or radiotherapy. Surgery, as well as attempting curative removal of tumours, may by excising endocrine glands alter the balance of hormones upon which the growth of some cancers seems to depend. All three modes of treatment can be used too as a means of palliation when cure is judged impossible or unlikely. Surgical operation can relieve symptoms due to pressure or obstruction; radiotherapy, chemotherapy, and hormone treatment will often abolish pain and may prolong comfortable and useful life. It is because of the many ways in which these therapeutic techniques can help in the cure or relief of patients with cancer that a co-operative approach to the problems of treatment is essential. Nevertheless radiotherapy and chemotherapy are powerful weapons, as capable of causing damage as they are of bringing benefit and it is seldom wise to prescribe them unless there are positive and well-defined reasons for their use. They should not be regarded in the light of the placebo — the bottle of harmless coloured medicine formerly given to a patient to convince him that he is receiving treatment.

A recent report on the use of interferon in the treatment of myelomatosis – a cancer of the bone-marrow – has aroused great interest. Interferon is a specific protective substance produced by cells infected experimentally with virus. Its effect is thought to be due to preventing the synthesis of one of the basic viral constituents, nucleic acid. Four patients suffering from myelomatosis were treated with interferon derived from human white blood cells. In two there was great improvement and the illness was arrested. In the other two all symptoms and signs disappeared and the disease appeared to be cured. In none has there been any suggestion of relapse or recurrence since treatment was discontinued several months ago.

If these results can be confirmed an entirely new approach to the treatment of cancer may be opening.

Many people with cancer have such symptoms of general ill-health as lethargy, loss of weight, nausea, sickness, and a failing appetite. These disappear when the malignant disease has been cured. Unhappily cure is not always attainable, the disease escapes from control, and health continues to deteriorate. Moreover effective treatment by surgery, radiotherapy, or chemotherapy is often a gruelling process and may leave the patient possibly cured, but certainly weak and exhausted. At all those times support is needed and this will include such mundane but important matters as regulation of bowel action, the provision of adequate and appropriate food, the supervision of sleep, rest, and exercise, and, above all, skilled nursing care. Sometimes blood transfusion is require to repair anaemia; sometimes when resistance, reduced by malignant disease or its treatment, is overwhelmed by infection, treatment with antibiotic drugs must be prescribed.

There are sadly too many occasions when hopes of cure fade and the disease can no longer be restrained; finally it becomes apparent to all, and often to the sick man himself, that the curtain has gone up on the last act. The problems of care in this stage have, of late, greatly exercised the minds of those responsible. The past few years have seen the estab-

Treatment

lishment of a number of hospices devoted to what has come to be called 'terminal' or 'continuing care' and valuable lessons have been learned from the devoted few who have worked in them. They have shown their colleagues how to relieve the symptoms, how to alleviate the fears and anxieties, and how to bring peace and comfort to those with only a few weeks of life remaining.

A problem often discussed in the popular press is whether a patient should be told when he is found to have cancer. It is a question to which there can be no categorical answer. Doctors are slowly coming to recognize that in general patients prefer to know the truth. There may indeed be some from whom it is best concealed, but they are few and it is exceptional to regret having told a patient that he has malignant disease. An all-important proviso is that suspicions should not be voiced and the diagnosis must be unshakeably established before it is revealed.

There can be no doubt that when prolonged treatment, whether by surgery, radiotherapy, or chemotherapy, is required, that patient must be told. Adequate treatment demands his full understanding co-operation and it is asking more than can be expected of any rational being to submit to a gruelling and protracted therapeutic programme without knowing the reason for it.

To conceal the facts is a mistaken kindness. It is often due to cowardice or embarrassment on the part of the doctor for no-one enjoys imparting bad news. The lie direct should be avoided in all circumstances. The sick man's suspicion that he is being kept in the dark is more likely to cause anxiety than the knowledge of what he has to face. Moreover, in the end the true position is always starkly revealed and, if it has been kept hidden from him he will feel unable to trust his family or his doctor thereafter. Even when cure is impossible, a transparent charade played by his relatives and his doctors is infinitely more painful than a gentle and sympathetic account of the true position. It establishes rapport and abolishes the distressing sense of isolation which is the inevitable result of the best-intentioned deception.

9

Cancer of the digestive system

The digestive system or alimentary tract starts at the mouth and ends at the anus. Throughout its length it is exposed to potential carcinogens which enter with the food or drink, but although many substances have fallen under suspicion few, if any, have been positively identified as a cause of cancer in man. Nevertheless all parts of the system are common sites of malignant disease except the small intestine, the relative freedom of which has never been adequately explained. In its upper reaches some difficulties of classification arise for there is an area from the back of the nose to the vocal cords which serves as a passage both for the air we breathe and for the food and drink we swallow. This is sometimes called the aero-digestive tract. Surgeons concerned with the treatment of tumours in this general region often describe themselves as specialists in 'head and neck' cancer.

Cancers of the mouth and throat

Cancers in this area, which includes the throat from the back of the nose to the vocal cords, account for some 2.2 per cent of all deaths from malignant disease in England and Wales. Almost all arise from the mucous membrane lining this passage and are carcinomas. There are a few rarities and the tonsil, which is much like a lymphatic gland, is prone to a form known as lymphoma (see Chapter 14).

There are several sites in the mouth or throat from which carcinomas arise. Registrations for the 4-year period 1963–6 show the tumours to have been distributed thus: lip 25 per cent, tongue 19 per cent, mouth and gums 25 per cent, area at the back of the nose (naso-pharynx) 6 per cent, and the rest of the throat, including the tonsils, 26 per cent. These areas are almost all more commonly affected in men. The

80

Cancer of the digestive system

single exception is the lower end of the throat where it joins the gullet. Here cancers are more common in women and often preceded by changes in the mucous membrane associated with anaemia due to lack of iron. All tumours in this area increase in frequency as age advances.

Figures for mortality are not of great value because, happily, the rate of cure is high. However, they give an indication of the changes which have taken place in incidence of these tumours. To take cancer of the tongue as an example: certified as dying from this disease per year per million living for the quinquennium 1911–15 there were 53 men and 5 women; by the period 1966–70 the numbers of men had fallen to 9 and of women had remained at 5. The mortality rates for 1975 are almost identical at males 8 and females 6. The increased frequency of cancer of the tongue with advancing years is borne out by the figures for age-adjusted registrations per 1 000 000 living: for those aged 40–44 it was 5 and for those aged 70–74, 84.

A number of factors play a part in the cause of these cancers. Countries in which the standard of living is low have the highest rates. Various irritants, swallowed, inhaled, or chewed, are clearly of importance. In those countries where it is the custom to smoke 'beedi' – sun-dried uncured tobacco wrapped in a dry leaf – cancer of the mouth and tongue is common. 'Reverse smoking', smoking with the lighted end of the cigar or cigarette inside the mouth, is thought to account for the relative frequency of cancer of the palate in India, Venezuela, and other countries where this habit is common. The chewing of tobacco mixed with lime or of betel nut accounts for the high incidence of cancer of the tongue in Bombay where the rate per 1 000 000 is 140 for men and 37 for women, compared with figures of 14 and 8 in England and Wales.

Cancer of the nasopharynx is a rare tumour in most parts of the world but common in natives of South China. In Chinese males in Hong Kong the incidence is 243 while in England and Wales it is only 6. This curious distribution has been discussed in Chapter 2. It is thought to have a genetic

81

basis, because the incidence in the Southern Chinese remains high after emigration, although it has recently been reported that in the American-born second generation of such emigrants the incidence is lower. Another curious finding is that a high proportion of persons with this tumour harbour the Epstein–Barr virus which is constantly present in African children with the Burkitt lymphoma and the probable cause of glandular fever. Whether its connection with nasopharyngeal cancer is causal or whether it is no more than that of a harmless bystander is unknown.

Prolonged irritation from ill-fitting dentures or from broken jagged teeth may lead to cancer and it has long been recognized that it may follow chronic inflammation of the surface of the tongue due to syphilis. It may well be that now adequate treatment of this infection explains much of the drop in its frequency. Cancer of the lip was attributed in the past to smoking a clay pipe. It is more common in the fair-skinned, particularly when living in a sunny climate such as Northern Australia or the southern United States.

Precancerous conditions of the mouth are common. One of these, leukoplakia, consists of white, thickened patches on the inside of the cheeks. In 8–12 per cent of persons with this condition cancer eventually develops. Many of the irritants described above lead to a thickening of the mucous membrane with scar-formation beneath it and this 'submucosal fibrosis' is also a forerunner of malignant change.

The form these cancers take varies with their point of origin. It may be a small nodule the size of a pea or less, it may be an ulcer with thickened edges, it may be a wart-like projection, or it may be a flat area of thickening. In most instances the tumour extends locally, at a rate varying greatly from one person to another. The more aggressive tumours soon become fixed to neighbouring tissues and spread rapidly to the lymphatic glands in the neck or under the chin. Sometimes an enlarged lymphatic gland in the neck, which biopsy proves to be cancerous, is the first sign of cancer in this region. Indeed, in some patients it may be difficult to locate the primary tumour which gave rise to it. Blood-borne metastases are rare and if the cancer proves lethal it is usually due to local causes, such as extension and ulceration of the primary tumour or of enlarged lymphatic glands in the neck. The closing event is often bronchopneumonia resulting from inhalation of infected material from the malignant ulcer.

In most instances the tumour is found early. The nodule, ulcer, or thickening is felt and medical advice is sought. There is often little or no pain in the early stages, but since much of the area is constantly moving, discomfort on eating or swallowing is common. Cancer of the tonsil often causes few symptoms until it has grown sufficiently to interfere with normal swallowing. Nasopharyngeal tumours again are silent until large enough to cause stuffiness of the nose, alter the voice by impeding the movement of the soft palate, or interfere with hearing by obstruction of the inner end of the Eustachian tube, leading from the middle compartment of the ear to the nasopharynx.

Enlarged lymphatic glands may be present even when the patient first visits his doctor. Their influence both upon treatment and upon the outlook is of the first importance. The lymphatic spread is often late with tumours of the mouth, lip, and nasopharynx. It is often early with cancer of the tonsil. With cancer of the tongue, enlarged glands are present when advice is first sought in 40 per cent of those in whom the tumour is on the front part of the tongue and in 60 per cent where it is at the back.

The diagnosis of cancer in the mouth or throat seldom presents difficulty. On the lip, the tongue, the palate, the cheeks, the gums, and the tonsils, the tumour can usually be easily seen and felt. When deeper in the throat an instrument may be required for an adequate view. Once suspicions have been raised it is essential to remove a fragment of tissue from the suspected area for microscopic examination. An area thought to be precancerous must be treated in the same way and, if study of the biopsy material does not establish the diagnosis of cancer, a watch must be kept and the biopsy repeated after an interval.

In the treatment of many of these tumours the choice between radiotherapy and surgery depends upon the extent of local spread. Often the consequences of surgery are so mutilating that radiotherapy, especially for a localized primary tumour, is to be preferred. When enlarged lymphatic glands are present, wide surgical excision is advisable provided they are not firmly fixed, for this means that the cancer has broken through the capsule of the gland and is infiltrating the neighbouring tissues. In such circumstances cure is not to be envisaged and palliative radiotherapy is the most that can be offered.

Surgery is indicated where the growth has invaded bone and this is common with cancer of the gum. It is advisable also if the tumour is known to be resistant to radiotherapy, when radiotherapy has failed, or when it has been followed by a recurrence of the growth. Cancers of the lip respond excellently to radiotherapy or to surgery.

Early cancers of the tongue are probably best treated by radiotherapy delivered by radium needles temporarily applied to the tongue itself. However the results of surgery are equally good and the disturbance of speech and of swallowing after removal of half the tongue is surprisingly little. Enlarged glands are often present; sometimes they are due to infection of the cancer and disappear after the primary tumour has been adequately treated; sometimes they indicate lymphatic spread. If it is possible to keep the patient under close observation the surgeon may consider it justifiable to wait and see whether the glands shrink after treatment of the primary growth. When observation is impossible or if they do not disappear excision of all the glands on the affected side of the neck is usually advised. When there has been extensive local spread, surgery is almost always required.

Cancers of the mouth and gums can usually be treated with radium needles but if bone has been invaded surgery is required. Radiotherapy may damage bone and be followed by intractable pain and an ulcerated area which will not heal. The surgeon will usually need to excise a part of the upper or lower jaw, but if all the tumour is removed healing is rapid and complete.

Cancer of the tonsil before it has invaded the lymphatic glands is best treated by radiotherapy and some follow this by removal of the tonsil. Cancer of the nasopharynx can only be dealt with by radiotherapy; spread to the lymphatic glands is usually late.

Chemotherapy has given some encouraging results and methods have been developed by which the anticancer drug is injected directly into the artery which supplies blood to the area of the tumour. This enables the full weight of the attack to be brought to bear directly on the growth. A combination of this form of chemotherapy with high-voltage radiotherapy holds promise as a useful method of treating advanced disease.

It is important that the possibilities of cure are assessed before treatment is started. Often this presents no difficulty. When there has been extensive spread to lymphatic glands, operation, even when possibly curative, is likely to be unacceptably mutilating. If the enlarged glands are anchored to the skin or to the tissues beneath them radiotherapy is unlikely to cure.

If cure is judged unattainable, relief of symptoms becomes the primary aim of treatment. Moderate doses of irradiation will often shrink enlarged glands and prevent their destroying the skin and causing malignant ulceration, but nursing care and relief of pain and discomfort are the paramount considerations.

The likelihood of cure depends upon the site of origin of the cancer and on the stage at which treatment is started. The presence of enlarged glands makes the outlook much less favourable. It is usual to express the rate of cure in those with malignant disease as the percentage of persons who are surviving at the end of 5 years from the date on which the diagnosis was established or the treatment started. For cancer of the lip the 5-year cure rate is 90 per cent. When it arises in the tongue the overall rate is 30 per cent, but for early cases it is as high as 70 per cent. It is far worse when the cancer originates at the back of the tongue. The 5-year cure rate for 'early' cancer of the tonsil is 50 per cent, but when enlarged glands are present it falls to 20 per cent; for cancers of the mouth and gums the figure for early cases is 70 per cent, but when glands are enlarged only 35 per cent, and for nasopharyngeal cancers the rates are 60 per cent or with enlarged glands 40 per cent.

Cancer of the oesophagus

Cancer of the oesophagus caused 2.7 per cent of all deaths from malignant disease in England and Wales in 1975. The proportion is a little greater in men at 2.9 per cent than in women at 2.6 per cent. The numbers certified as dying from this disease in 1975 were 1886 men and 1484 women. The results of treatment are so unsuccessful that there is little difference between figures for incidence and those for mortality. For the period 1911–15 the death rate per year per 1 000 000 living was 64 for men and 20 for women, for 1966–70 the figures were men 67 and women 50, and for the year 1975 men 79 and women 59. Thus this form of malignant disease is becoming more common: in males the last 65 years have shown an increase in death rate of 22 per cent, but in women the rise has been almost 200 per cent. The reason for this is not clear: women are especially prone to cancer of the upper end of the oesophagus and it is possible that some of these have been regarded previously as arising at the lower end of the throat and thus classified as cancer of the pharynx. It is a disease seldom seen below the age of 50 years and occurs most often in the sixth or seventh decades.

The curious geographical variations in its incidence have been mentioned in Chapter 2 together with the reasons for believing that in part genetic causes must be responsible. That such factors can be of importance is shown by its association with a warty thickening of the palms and soles called tylosis. This is a rare disorder which runs in families; amonst 45 members of affected families 18 had cancer of the oesophagus.

Carcinogens taken with food or drink may well be important. An association with alcohol and tobacco has long been claimed and is said to explain the incidence of 294 per 1 000 000 in the French department of L'Ille et Vilaine. A great increase in the incidence of this cancer has been reported in the Bantu. It began when a change was made from brewing native maize beer in earthenware vessels to using galvanized drums. The suggestion has been made that the drums contained a carcinogen not previously present, but efforts to isolate it have been unsuccessful. It has also become more common in Chinese men. Many explanations for this have been put forward, including the suggestion that Chinese men eat their food very hot while the women are forced to wait until their menfolk are sated by which time it has become cold.

There are one or two diseases of the oesophagus with which cancer is more often associated than can be attributed to chance. Achalasia of the cardia is an uncommon disorder in which the muscles of the lower end of the oesophagus fail to relax normally due to a disturbance of the nervous mechanism which controls them. In one series of persons dying who had had achalasia, nearly one-third were found to have cancer of the oesophagus. Malignant changes may supervene upon the scarring caused by swallowing corrosive fluids such as lysol. The association of cancer of the upper end of the oesophagus with anaemia due to lack of iron in women has been discussed. It is preceded by precancerous changes in this area which cause difficulty in swallowing and this combination is known as the Plummer–Vinson syndrome. Claims have been made that cancer of the oesophagus occurs more frequently than expected in those with a hiatus hernia. In this condition a part of the stomach bulges into the chest through the opening in the diaphragm which normally accommodates the oesphagus. Hiatus hernia is an exceedingly common disorder and there is no support for these claims.

There are three sites in the oesophagus in which cancer commonly arises. The first is at the upper end, or post-cricoid region, where some 15 per cent of tumours occur; the second is roughly in the middle where 35–50 per cent are found; and finally those arising at the lower end amount to 35–50 per cent. The post-cricoid growths occur chiefly in women as mentioned previously. Those at the lower end of the oesophagus are not easily distinguished from cancers arising at the upper end of the stomach. The importance of this distinction is not as academic as it sounds because the two tumours behave very differently.

A cancer of the oesophagus grows rapidly, spreading round the circumference of the gullet to narrow or even block the passage completely. The outer surface of the oesophagus is not covered by a membrane in the way the peritoneum covers the intestines. The barrier this imposes to local extension of the growth is therefore lacking and the cancer rapidly penetrates the wall of the gullet spreading to the lymphatic glands running alongside it within the chest. Later there is blood-borne spread commonly leading to metastases in the liver and lungs.

The earliest symptoms of cancer of the oesophagus is almost invariably difficulty in swallowing with a sense of food being arrested in the gullet at a level which can be accurately located. The difficulty is at first for solid food and particularly meat. Occasionally in the early stages it is intermittent, but it soon becomes persistent and even to drink water is difficult and painful.

The result is starvation with rapid loss of weight and strength. After a while symptoms due to local extension ensue. The growth may ulcerate and destroy an area of the gullet's wall so that infection spreads into the chest and pneumonia results. Finally metastases in the lung or liver may appear and determine the issue.

The last entry in the diary of John Casaubon, a surgeon of Canterbury, in 1691 describes the symptoms with a vivid pathos:

88

Cancer of the digestive system

'At dinner I was almost Choaked by swallowing a bit of Roasted Sl. of mutton which as I thought stuck in the passage about the mouth of the Stomach . . . and on a sudden I grew lean as a Skeleton and at some tymes very faint and feeble, although I recovered in some measure and had Stomach 2 eate, my meate Doeth me no gt. good and I am in a Kind of Atrophie'.

Diagnosis seldom presents a problem. The difficulty in swallowing is an immediate indication for a barium X-ray examination of the oesophagus. This reveals an abnormality in 94 per cent of cases, but proof is essential and the next step must be for a surgeon to pass an oesophagoscope which will allow him to inspect the mucous membrane lining the gullet and to remove a small piece of tissue from the suspicious area for microscopic examination. Even when the X-ray examination shows no abnormality, if the difficulty in swallowing persists, oesophagoscopy is advisable.

Treatment is unsatisfactory. Surgery presents immense technical difficulties. In 50 per cent the growth has spread to the lymphatic glands in the vicinity and is thus unsuitable for operation. Of those in whom surgical exploration is considered justifiable in between only 20 and 40 per cent does the surgeon find himself able to remove the growth. At the upper end of the oesophagus the inevitable mutilation makes surgery almost impossible to accept and the reconstruction necessary offers virtually insuperable difficulties. The technical problems encountered with cancers of the middle part of the gullet are little less. Only growths at the lower end are likely to be suitable for operation and here too great expertise is required. The average death rate immediately after operation is about 20 per cent and the ultimate results of surgical treatment are profoundly depressing. The chances of being alive after 5 years are 13 per cent when the growth is in the middle part of the oesophagus and 6 per cent when at the lower end.

Radiotherapy offers as good a chance of cure as surgery and possibly better when the growth is at the upper end of the oesophagus. At one centre the 5-year survival after irradiation was 17 per cent while only 1 in 9 persons undergoing surgery were still alive after that time. Claims have been made for a 20 per cent 5-year survival for this type of cancer treated by radiotherapy irrespective of its site, and the best surgery can offer is 11 per cent. These claims are contested, but it is certain that at present no clear case exists for surgery in the upper end of mid-oesophageal tumours.

Because local spread of this disease is so early and so rapid treatment is as often concerned with palliation as with cure. The most distressing symptom is the difficulty in swallowing and this can usually be relieved, at any rate for a while, by radiotherapy in doses less than those used when cure is attempted. Various tubes have been devised which can be placed in the oesophagus at the level of the growth to keep the passage open. They are seldom satisfactory. In past times an artificial opening into the stomach was often made by the surgeon and the patient fed through a tube into this. This is mentioned only to be condemned: although preventing death from starvation, it does no more than ensure a protracted course of misery, pain, and discomfort.

The outlook at present for those with cancer of the oesophagus can only be described as disastrous. It is difficult to see how the results of surgical treatment can be improved and it is probable that the treatment of choice is radiotherapy. Chemotherapy as yet has had little impact on the disease, but there is hope that it may, in combination with radiotherapy, offer a prospect less dismal than the present one.

Cancer of the stomach

Until the recent increase in cancer of the lung, cancer of the stomach, judged from its frequency as a cause of death, was the commonest form of malignant disease in the United Kingdom. For the quinquennium 1911–15 it was responsible for 16.7 per cent of all deaths certified as due to cancer; for men the proportion was 20 per cent and for women 14 per cent. Since then its frequency has declined not only relative

Cancer of the digestive system

to other cancers but also in absolute numbers. In 1975, 11 983 persons in England and Wales were certified as dying from cancer of the stomach, or 9.8 per cent of all deaths from malignant disease. The figures for men were 6983 or 10.6 per cent and for women 5000 or 8.8 per cent. The mortality rate shows a similar change. The number of deaths per year from this cause per 1 000 000 living for the period 1911–15 were 201 men and 171 women. By the period 1951–5 the figures had risen to 378 and 275; by 1966–70 they had fallen to 314 and 222. Men are affected more commonly than women. Overall the proportions are seven women for every ten men: in middle age it is between two and three times more common in men, but in old age the proportions become almost equal. It is essentially a disease of the second half of life: the age-adjusted death rates per 1 000 000 living per year are 32 men and 16 women aged 35–44 and 2432 and 1371 for those aged 75–84. The decrease in the death rate in the United States has been even more striking than in this country having fallen from 290 per year per 1 000 000 living for men and 220 for women in 1967. The explanation for this decline has so far eluded even the most ingenious.

It would be reasonable to suppose that of all organs the stomach was most likely to be at the mercy of carcinogens taken in with food and drink. Nevertheless no substance has ever been convincingly inculpated. Cereals, smoked and fried foods have been found innocent. Tobacco and alcohol have been blamed as much as a matter of principle, rather than on more solid evidence. It is suggested that cancer of the stomach is more common in the lower socio-economic groups. It is abnormally frequent in Japan where the death rate was 680 for men and 370 for women for 1964–5, compared with 230 and 110 for England and Wales and 90 and 40 for white Americans. High figures are also reported from Chile. In neither instance has an explanation been found although it has been suggested that the drinking of sake and eating of contaminated soya bean flour might account for some of the increase in Japanese. It seems established that when Japanese emigrate the frequency of cancer of the stomach diminishes progressively the longer they live abroad. This suggests that a carcinogen is responsible and that the increase is not of genetic cause.

Other causal relationships are few and uncertain. It was thought to be more common in males of blood group A, but this is now uncertain. There is little doubt that it is more likely to occur in patients with pernicious anaemia than in the previously healthy. In this anaemia there is a thinning of the lining membrane of the stomach with a disappearance of many of the glands it normally contains and which make the digestive juices. This has been regarded as a precancerous change, but the risk of cancer is only some three times greater than normal. Chronic inflammation of the stomach lining–chronic gastritis–does not appear to predispose to cancer and indeed is an ill-defined disorder. For many years arguments have raged over the chances of a simple gastric ulcer becoming malignant. It has never been firmly established that this change even occurs and opinion is now opposed to the possibility.

The form taken by a cancer of the stomach is variable. It may present as a tumour, projecting into the stomach as a 'polyp' and this in due course will ulcerate and bleed or it may appear first as an ulcer which slowly extends. Rarely it will infiltrate the stomach wall without actual tumour or ulcer until it has spread throughout the whole organ to cause what is called 'leathern-bottle stomach'. About half the cancers arise at the further end of the stomach, near the exit; some 40 per cent start in the middle and the remainder at the upper end where the gullet enters. In almost every case the cells from which the cancer arise are those of the glands in the lining of the stomach and it is therefore what the pathologists class as an adenocarcinoma. A few other rare forms of malignant tumour are occasionally encountered.

When the cancer advances it may spread directly to invade other organs in the neighbourhood. These include the liver and the pancreas. Sometimes it passes through the wall of the stomach to reach its outer surface and cells may be shed and become implanted on the membrane covering the abdominal contents, the peritoneum, or in other organs within the abdominal cavity, most frequently the ovaries. Occasionally the spread is of the 'leathern-bottle' type described above. Metastases form early in lymphatic glands, especially those in the vicinity of the stomach itself. Sometimes the first indication of disease is an enlarged gland behind the left collar bone or in the left armpit. Blood-borne secondary deposits form in the liver and elsewhere, often in bone.

The symptoms of gastric cancer depend upon where in the stomach the tumour arises. They are often insidious and perhaps the most common is indigestion. At first this is a vague sense of discomfort which leads to belching in the hopes of procuring relief; later the discomfort becomes more severe, amounting in due course to pain; it is accompanied by a feeling of distension. The appetite is easily satisfied and gradually fades until there is a revulsion against food and particularly against meat. In consequence there is rapid loss of weight. If the tumour arises at the further end of the stomach it will obstruct and finally block the exit, leading to vomiting which is often copious. The material vomited may contain traces of bright blood, but is more usually coloured a dark brown from blood altered by the gastric juices, and traditionally likened to coffee grounds. If the growth is near the entrance of the gullet, the symptoms may resemble those of cancer of the oesophagus with difficulty in swallowing and a feeling that food is held up at the level of the lower end of the breast bone. In addition to these symptoms, slow loss of blood from the ulcerated surface of the growth will inevitably lead to anaemia.

The diagnosis of cancer of the stomach seldom offers difficulty when its possibility is considered. Unhappily the early symptoms are so indefinite that advice is seldom sought until the disease is advanced and has spread beyond the confines of the organ. It is rarely possible on physical examination to feel a tumour, but, when it is, the cancer is almost certainly so far advanced that cure is impossible.

When suspicions of the diagnosis are aroused a barium meal X-ray is usually the first step. An experienced radiologist will be able to identify a cancer in about 90 per cent of cases. If this is indeterminate, the interior of the stomach can be inspected through a gastroscope. The fibre-optic instrument allows the whole of the mucous membrane lining the organ to be examined and a biopsy made from any suspicious areas. In some cases cancer cells can be identified in the stomach juices obtained by passing a stomach tube. The final court of appeal is for a surgeon to explore the abdomen and examine the stomach directly. This is essential if suspicions are aroused either by radiology or gastroscopy. There are times when it is justifiable even when the radiologist and the gastroscopist have found nothing amiss.

The only chance of cure of gastric cancer is given by radical surgery. The operation entails removal of two-thirds of the stomach, or in some cases the entire organ. The remaining part of the stomach or the lower end of the gullet is joined to a loop of upper small intestine to restore the continuity of the digestive tract. Between 75 and 90 per cent of those found to have a cancer of the stomach are suitable for surgical exploration and in some 50–60 per cent of those explored it is possible to undertake the radical operation described above. The whole stomach has to be removed when the growth is at its upper end: the operation is one of considerable magnitude and carries a death rate of about 20 per cent. When only two-thirds of the organ require removal the mortality of the operation falls to 10 per cent.

The figures for cure vary with the centre making the report. When the cancer is confined to the stomach and has not spread to the lymphatic glands some 57 per cent survive over 5 years. In only 10–15 per cent is the growth found at operation found to be limited. When the growth has penetrated to the outer coat of the stomach, but the glands invaded are only those in its immediate neighbourhood the

Cancer of the digestive system

5-year survival may still reach 38 per cent. Of all those who undergo radical operation some 25–30 per cent are living after 5 years. It is a disheartening fact that there has been little or no change in these figures for several decades and this underlines the need for a fresh approach to the treatment of this disease.

Once the impossibility of cure has been established deterioration is usually rapid: the average survival is no more than 7½ months and half have died in 4 months. The problems of palliation are many. When there is constant vomiting due to obstruction to the outlet of the stomach it is difficult to decide whether an operation to relieve it is a kindness. The patient will live perhaps a few months longer and possibly die in a fashion which is no more comfortable. Obstruction at the upper end of the stomach raises the problems discussed under cancer of the oesophagus.

There is little agreement over the part chemotherapy should play. It certainly cannot cure cancer of the stomach. Thus if it has a value it is a palliative one. The place of radiotherapy is even more debatable. Gastric cancer is radioresistant: irradiating the abdomen causes the distressing symptoms of radiation sickness and is of little palliative value. It is useful in relieving the pain of metastases in bone, but for little else.

Claims have been made for a combination of chemotherapy and radiotherapy. In a small series those so treated lived an average of 14 months while those who received no specific treatment only survived 6 months. Such results offer some encouragement to the research worker, but at present little consolation to the sufferer from gastric cancer.

Cancer of the bowel

Cancer of the small intestine is rare and when it does occur it usually takes the form of lymphoma (see Chapter 14). By contrast, the large intestine is a common site for malignant disease and 98 per cent arise from cells of glands lying in the inner coat of the bowel. They are in pathological terms adenocarcinomas. The remaining 2 per cent are made up of lymphomas and sarcomas.

The large bowel starts low down on the right hand side of the abdomen, ascends to a position just below the liver, takes a right-angled turn across the abdomen to the area deep to the lower ribs on the left side. Here it takes another right-angled turn to descend to low on the left side where an S-shaped bend (the sigmoid colon) brings it to the final section, or rectum, which reaches the surface at the anus. Cancers of the colon and rectum are usually considered separately because the problems they present to the surgeon are dissimilar and because they show other differences to which reference is made later.

Cancers of the large bowel were responsible for 13.5 per cent of deaths due to malignant disease in England and Wales in 1975. Deaths certified as due to cancer of the colon in that year amounted to 4245 males and to 6269 women and the mortality rates were respectively 177 and 248. The figures for persons certified as dying from cancer of the rectum were men 3231 and women 2836, and the mortality rates 135 and 113. This preponderance of female deaths from colonic cancer has been noted for many years. The mortality rates of this disease have changed: for the 5-year period 1931–5 rates for cancer of the colon were 174 for men and 200 for women. In men they rose up to the period 1941–5 and then fell until 1966–70 when the rate was 169. In women the mortality rate reached 264 for the quinquennium 1946–50, fell to 232 in 1966–70, and for 1975 was 248. The mortality rates for cancer of the rectum show similar variations. For men in the quinquennia indicated they were 1911–15, 96; 1941–5, 185; 1966–70, 131; and for 1975, 135. In women the figures were 1911–15, 71; 1946–50, 113; 1966–70, 109; and 1975, 113. Thus in men the frequency of rectal cancer as a cause of death has declined since the 1940s, whereas in women it has remained unchanged.

The proportion of cancers of the large intestine which can be cured is high and thus the mortality figures quoted above

Cancer of the digestive system

give an inexact measure of the incidence of the disease. In the period 1963–6 the number of persons per year per 1 000 000 living registered as suffering from cancer of the colon were 180 males and 233 females, and of cancer of the rectum 163 males and 130 females. The probable inaccuracy of these figures for incidence has already been noted. In other Western nations and in the United States the incidence of cancer of the large bowel is also high. On the other hand in the underdeveloped countries the incidence is suprisingly low. It has been noted that where cancer of the stomach is common, cancer of the large bowel is rare and vice versa. In those countries in which it is common it affects the higher socio-economic groups more than the lower. In the United Kingdom cancer of the colon has an unexpectedly high incidence in Scotland and north-west England. Like most forms of malignant disease it is rare below the age of 35 years and becomes progressively more common with advancing age.

There are a number of precancerous states which may precede cancer of the large bowel. Benign fleshy outgrowths known as polyps arising from the lining of the bowel are of frequent occurrence. They may cause no symptoms or they may bleed. They are often small and there has been debate over the frequency with which malignant disease ensues. In one rare type called the villous polyp cancer follows in 40 per cent. The hereditary disorder called familial polyposis of the colon has already been mentioned. In this disease many polyps are present throughout the length of the bowel and malignant change occurs in every case after a longer or shorter time. Often cancer arises in more than one area. The third precancerous state which requires mention is ulcerative colitis. It is a disease in which there is ulceration of the colon and the rectum causing diarrhoea and bleeding. It runs a prolonged course, the symptoms waxing and waning in severity and sometimes remitting for long periods. Malignant change is liable to occur when the disease extends throughout the entire length of the colon and increases with the passage

97

of time. It is estimated that in one with a 35-year history of ulcerative colitis the risk of cancer is 45 per cent. In half the patients cancerous change occurs in more than one area of the colon.

With the exception of these precancerous states the cause of cancer of the large bowel is unknown. There are many points which suggest that a carcinogen taken in with the food or drink is likely. It has been noted that when Japanese, born in Japan where the incidence of cancer of the colon is low, emigrate to Hawaii, they develop the increased liability to the disease characteristic of the indigenous inhabitants. The possible association with diet, and especially with the protective effect of a high-residue diet, has been noted in Chapter 2. It has been suggested that bacterial action in the bowel may give rise to carcinogenic agents and this is more likely to occur when there is constipation and the contents of the bowel pass more slowly through the colon.

The position, as so often in malignant disease, is not clear cut. Genetic factors must not be overlooked. Excluding familial polyposis it has been found that there is some tendency for this disease to run in families and that when this is so multiple cancers of the colon are more common than where no relative is affected.

The different parts of the large intestine differ in their liability to malignant disease. The proportion of cancers found in the different regions of the colon are as follows: right ascending part 15 per cent; transverse section 5 per cent; descending left part 5 per cent; sigmoid colon 40 per cent; while 35 per cent occur in the rectum. Some 2.5 per cent of persons affected are found to have cancers in two or more sites. The importance of this distribution is that three-quarters of the cancers lie within reach of the examining finger or of an instrument (sigmoidoscope) through which the lower bowel can be examined.

The cancer may take the form of a fleshy swelling which protrudes into the intestine or it may form a malignant ulcer which spreads round its circumference leading to

Cancer of the digestive system

reduction in its calibre. The manner in which the cancer spreads depends upon its position. It may extend through the bowel wall and invade organs in the vicinity. This is more likely to occur with cancer of the rectum because of its close proximity to the bladder, the vagina, and the nerves leaving the lower end of the spinal cord. Spread to the lymphatic glands which lie alongside the bowel is early and soon extends to those at a greater distance. Cancer of the rectum may lead early to enlarged glands in the groin. It is reported that spread to the glands near the growth is found at operation in 40–70 per cent of cases. Finally, blood-borne secondary deposits are common especially in the liver and the lung, although they may occur in any organ or tissue.

Early symptoms of cancer of the large intestine are often slight and misleading. Vague abdominal discomfort is not replaced by pain until the disease is far advanced. A change in bowel habit is common, a symptom which must always be taken seriously in the middle-aged and elderly. Regularity may be replaced by constipation or by constipation alternating with bouts of diarrhoea. Those with cancer of the rectum often complain that after passing a motion they have a sense of incomplete evacuation. The only gross disturbance of function possible is an interference with the onward passage of the bowel contents. This is less likely to happen when the cancer is in the right half of the bowel for its contents are fluid and its calibre large. Obstruction of the bowel brings the patient to the doctor complaining of obstinate constipation, increasing distension, and perhaps vomiting. This is the opening event in 28 per cent of those with cancer of the right side, but in 40 per cent when on the left. The growth will often bleed and then lead to anaemia, but haemorrhage is rarely profuse and recognizable blood is seldom to be seen in the motion unless the cancer is in the rectum.

The early diagnosis essential to effective treatment is impossible unless advice is sought early. In a number of reported series the average time between noting the first symptom and the first consultation varied from 5 to 18 months. At the first consultation a mass can be felt in the abdomen in between 70 and 80 per cent of those with cancer of the right half of the colon, but in only 30–45 per cent of those in whom it is on the left. The examining finger or the sigmoidoscope is able to detect three-quarters of rectal cancers. If a tumour can be seen or felt the next step is to establish its nature. At the lower end of the bowel it can be inspected through a sigmoidoscope and a biopsy taken. If higher, X-ray examination after injection of barium into the bowel (barium enema) will show its exact position and usually provide adequate reason for surgical exploration (see Plate 2). Colonoscopy is not likely to be helpful, because when there is a bowel tumour exploration is almost always essential.

If symptoms raise suspicions of bowel cancer, but physical examination reveals no abnormality, further investigations are necessary. Tests of the motions for blood are useful for if they are positive the need to look further is reinforced; however, they may be negative in as many as 50 per cent of patients even when there is anaemia. Sigmoidoscopy is the first step and if this reveals nothing abnormal then a barium enema examination must follow. This calls for considerable expertise, but when it is available at least 90 per cent of cancers are detected. If suspicions remain in spite of a negative result from X-ray examination, colonoscopy is required. With the fibre-optic colonoscope the whole length of the bowel can be examined and material taken for pathological examination. It is a tedious process alike for patient and doctor, and requires an experienced observer of whom at present there are few.

A common diagnostic problem is the discovery on X-ray examination of a polyp in the colon. It can often be removed through the colonoscope and the question of its malignancy answered confidently. The likelihood of it being cancerous can be judged from its size. A polyp less than 0.5 centimetres in diameter has a 0.5 per cent chance of being malignant; when it is 3.5 centimetres or more in diameter this risk rises to 29 per cent.

Cancer of the digestive system

The only treatment which can offer cure to the sufferer from cancer of the large bowel is surgical excision of the tumour. Operation for relief of acute intestinal obstruction is an essential preliminary when this is the presenting symptom and excision of the growth has to await recovery from this complication.

In the absence of obstruction it is customary to excise the cancer and a length of bowel above and below it so that any glands in its immediate neighbourhood are removed. The continuity of the bowel is restored by joining up the two cut ends of the bowel. The exact nature of the operation varies with the site of the growth. If it is on the right side, the right half of the colon has to be removed because the anatomy of the blood supply makes it impossible to excise a shorter segment without endangering that left behind. On the left side excision of a lesser length of bowel can be safely undertaken. In the sigmoid colon and the upper part of the rectum a similar operation is possible, but in the lower part it is necessary to remove the whole rectum. This necessitates making an artificial opening, known as a colostomy, on to the skin of the abdomen through which the bowel can discharge its contents. The thought of a colostomy horrifies and distresses all patients. It is, of course, paramount that the possible need for it be explained before the operation. Nowadays its competent management after operation is the rule and patients are given instructions before leaving hospital by nurses specially trained for the purpose. There is an association of patients who themselves have had colostomies and are prepared to see and reassure those in whom it may be necessary explaining that its care is simple and that it is no bar to normal social existence and a full active life.

The results of operation have improved steadily. Of those judged suitable for surgery in 1932 curative operation proved possible in only 47 per cent and the death rate following surgery was 13 per cent; by 1957 the proportion in whom radical surgery was possible had risen to 93 per cent and the operative mortality had fallen to 3.8 per cent. In a large number of published series the operative mortality for cancer of the colon varied between 2 and 7 per cent with an average of 3.5 per cent and for cancer of the rectum between 2.4 and 8.7 per cent with an average of 4.1 per cent.

Cancer of the large bowel was one of the first malignant diseases in which an attempt was made to forecast the outcome of operation by grading the extent of spread of the tumour. In type A the cancer is limited to the mucous membrane lining the bowel and has not spread to invade the layer of muscle beneath it nor the lymphatic glands. In type B the muscle layer has been invaded, but not the lymphatic glands. In type C the disease has spread to the lymphatic glands. Using this grading the 5-year survivals for type A cancers is 61–81 per cent, for type B 25–64 per cent, and type C 6–28 per cent. The figures are the highest and lowest for a large number of series published by different surgeons.

Complications after operation are common: they occur more often when the cancer is of the rectum than when it is at a higher level. They include all the problems which may follow surgery, but infection is rather more frequent. Cystitis and difficulty in passing water often follow operation for rectal cancer and in a proportion of men impotence is a sequel.

Radiotherapy has been widely exploited in treatment. It has been used before operation with a view to shrinking the growth and thus facilitating surgery. Claims of up to 43 per cent increase in survival rates are made, but most surgeons remain unconvinced. There is little evidence that the figures are improved by routine post-operative treatment. It has been used when surgery is not feasible and in a large series treated with 'curative' doses of irradiation the mean 5-year survival was 6.4 per cent. It is prescribed even more extensively as a palliative treatment and will often achieve relief of symptoms, sometimes for as long as 5 years. Against this must be set the discomfort heavy irradiation of the lower abdomen entails with nausea, vomiting, and often irritation of the bowel and bladder.

102

Cancer of the digestive system

Attempts have been made to treat superficial cancer of the rectum (type A) by local destructive methods such as electro-coagulation, or by direct application of radium. The reports are unconvincing.

The place of radiotherapy in palliation has been mentioned. It has been used too with this aim in combination with chemotherapy, particularly with a drug called 5-fluorouracil. In a small series of patients with advanced disease half of those treated by radiotherapy alone lived 10½ months, and half of those receiving radiotherapy and 5-fluorouracil lived 16 months. Again, these figures can reasonably encourage the research workers but offer little solace to the man with cancer. Chemotherapy with 5-fluorouracil alone can sometimes prolong life. In one series patients were divided into those who showed no improvement with the drug and those who showed some, non-responders and responders. Non-responders survived for an average of 7 months, the same length of time as untreated patients; responders for an average of 17 months.

The final stages of cancer of the rectum which has recurred locally can be distressingly painful; the tumour may fill the pelvis, infiltrate the many nerves which lie there, and interfere with the working of the bladder. Much ingenuity is needed to control pain and operation to sever the nerve fibres in the spinal cord which carry the pain sensations to the brain is sometimes the only effective measure.

Cancer of the salivary glands

The salivary glands make the saliva which lubricates the mouth and starts the process of digestion. Malignant disease of these glands is rare and the only form which deserves mention is that arising in the parotid glands. These glands are familiar to all because of their swelling in patients with mumps. The reported annual incidence of this cancer per 1 000 000 living for 1963–66 was 120 for men and 130 for women. In 1975, 107 men and 56 women were certified as dying from cancer of salivary glands and the mortality rates were 4.45 and 2.2

Eighty-five per cent of salivary gland cancers arise in the parotid glands.

Benign tumours of the gland are some six times more common than malignant. They grow slowly over years and in a proportion malignant changes develop insidiously, often after a long period. In other instances the tumour is clearly malignant from its first appearance. From the pathological point of view these cancers are often bizarre because two types of cell, one lining the ducts in the gland and the other forming the saliva, make up the tumours. For this reason they are often described as 'mixed'.

Enlargement of a parotid gland is easily detected, but it is less easy to be certain at first glance whether the swelling is due to a growth or an inflammation, and still more difficult to decide whether it is benign or malignant. The cancers tend to grow more rapidly, are harder, and more firmly fixed. The facial nerve passes through the parotid gland; in one-third of cancers it is damaged and paralysis of the muscles of the face on the side of the tumour results. A 'needle' biopsy will often allow a definite diagnosis of cancer to be made.

It is generally considered advisable to remove all parotid tumours. Those that are benign are unsightly and may undergo malignant change: moreover it is not always easy to be certain that they are innocent. Unless their removal is meticulously complete benign tumours are liable to recur. If the tumour is clearly malignant an extensive operation is often necessary. It is usually impossible to spare the facial nerve, so the operation is likely to be followed by paralysis of that side of the face. This can often be remedied by a nerve graft.

The outlook varies with the pathological variety of the tumour. The 5-year survival overall is about 50 per cent: in the highly malignant types it is as low as 20 per cent, and in the indolent forms as high as 80 per cent.

Cancer of the pancreas

The pancreas is a gland responsible for much of the digestive juice. It lies high on the back wall of the abdomen. It consists of a head, lying just to the right of the midline and in contact with the duodenum; a body which rests on the tissues covering the front of the spinal column; and a tail stretching out to the left.

In 1975 cancer of the pancreas was the certified cause of death of 2963 men and of 2607 women: the mortality rates for this year were respectively 124 and 103. There has been a steady rise in its frequency over the last 70 years. The annual death rate for the quinquennium 1911–15 was 18 for men and 16 for women. It now ranks as the fifth most common fatal cancer.

The cause of pancreatic cancer remains completely unknown. It is accompanied by gall stones more often than would be expected, but there is no other clue. Smoking has been claimed as a causative factor but the evidence is unconvincing.

Eighty-five per cent of cancers of the pancreas are adenocarcinomas. In all varieties there is early spread to regional and other more distant lymphatic glands. Over one-half of those with this disease have secondary deposits in the liver when they first consult their doctors; in one-third the stomach or the duodenum has been invaded by the tumour and in more than a quarter it has spread to the surface of the gland. Metastases in bones and lungs are common and may cause symptoms before the primary growth declares itself.

The symptoms of cancer of the pancreas depend upon the part of the gland in which it originates, but there is often vague ill-health, loss of weight, and irregularity of bowel action before more clear-cut symptoms appear. In three-quarters of cases the cancer arises in the head of the organ and as it spreads it blocks the duct which carries the bile from the liver to the bowel. This results in bile seeping back into the blood stream and causing the yellow discoloration of the skin and whites of the eyes familiar as jaundice. Bile is also passed in the urine which becomes mahogany-brown in colour and, as it is prevented from reaching the bowel, the colour it normally gives to the motions is lost and they are pale grey resembling clay. Pain is a feature of all forms of pancreatic cancer, but particularly when it arises in the body of the organ. It may be felt just above the navel and come and go irregularly; more characteristic is a severe boring pain in the centre of the small of the back often worse at night and often eased by sitting up and bending forward.

Other symptoms include repeated clotting in small veins, sometimes in the legs, sometimes in the arms. In between 10 and 20 per cent of those with cancer of the pancreas there is diabetes mellitus. The cells which make insulin lie in the substance of the pancreas. Thus it is also a gland of internal secretion. It is unknown whether the cancer causes the diabetes mellitus by destroying these cells or whether the diabetes in some way predisposes to cancer of the organ.

The diagnosis of cancer of the pancreas, especially when it does not cause jaundice, is often of great difficulty. Early symptoms are indeterminate and all investigations often prove negative. In less than a quarter can a tumour be felt; it lies in the abdomen between the navel and the lower end of the breast bone. Often the liver is enlarged by secondary deposits when the paitent first seeks medical advice. More often, however, no explanation can be found for the patient's obvious ill-health. Once suspicion is aroused a barium meal X-ray may provide evidence because the tumour sometimes presses upon the duodenum, the section of small bowel immediately beyond the stomach and wrapped round the head of the pancreas. However it is often unhelpful.

Arteriography may show an abnormal pattern of the blood vessels in the pancreas: but it is a technically difficult and tedious method. An isotopic scan will sometimes outline a tumour in the organ. All these methods are uncertain, but recently it has proved possible with the aid of the fibre-optic endoscope to pass a tube into the pancreatic duct through which radio-opaque fluid can be injected. X-rays taken after this procedure will usually define a tumour.

Cancer of the digestive system

Probably computerized axial tomography will prove the most certain and valuable method of diagnosis and it has the additional advantage of being 'non-invasive'. Cancer cells can often be found in the pancreatic juices drawn off through a tube passed into the pancreatic duct.

Cancer cells can often be found in the pancreatic juices drawn off through a tube passed into the pancreatic duct. When these two methods are used it is claimed that a diagnostic accuracy of 95 per cent can be achieved.

The treatment of cancer of the pancreas is beset with difficulties. It is insensitive to radiotherapy and has shown little response to treatment with drugs. It follows that complete removal of the tumour by operation offers the only hope of cure. However in more than half the persons presenting with this disease the cancer has spread to the lymphatic glands in its neighbourhood and to the liver, making cure impossible. The operation to remove the tumour is one of formidable magnitude, demanding rare expertise; it carries a considerable mortality and the post-operative period is always stormy and frequently punctuated by grave complications. Until recently these considerations have discouraged all but the most adventurous surgeons, but of late a rather more optimistic attitude has become apparent. Earlier published figures showed that in less than 1 in 5 was removal of the tumour possible, that the operation itself was fatal in one-quarter of these, and that one-half suffered major complications. There has been a move in favour of removal of the whole pancreas, in place of the previous operation where there was partial removal of the gland, together with the duodenum. In skilled hands the operative mortality has been halved and in one small series one-quarter were living after 3 years. Depressing though these figures are, they are an advance on any results published before and encourage efforts to achieve earlier diagnosis.

In at least half of the patients with this disease palliation is all that can be offered. The course of the illness is often short: in one series reported half lived 10½ months from the first symptoms and from the time the diagnosis was established the average survival was 6 months, half being dead within 3½ months.

When jaundice is present an operation to by-pass the obstruction to the bile duct often brings great relief and on an average prolongs survival from 2 months to 4½ months. Radiotherapy has nothing to offer and the same is true of chemotherapy, although careful studies of those treated with a combination of the two showed that the survival time could be prolonged from 6 to 10 months. For the rest, relief of pain and the control of other symptoms make considerable demands on the skill of the physician.

Cancer of the liver

Primary cancer of the liver is a rare disease in the United Kingdom. It must be distinguished from the common secondary cancer in which the liver is the seat of secondary deposits of cancers arising primarily in other organs. In 1975 primary liver cancer caused the deaths of 352 men and 211 women in England and Wales. The mortality rate was 15 for men and 8 for women. The ratio of men to women was 1:0.6 and it accounted for 0.46 per cent of deaths certified as due to malignant disease. It is somewhat more common in the United States where it makes up 0.75 per cent of fatal cancers. Its frequency has increased slightly.

In some parts of the world primary cancer of the liver is one of the commonest of malignant tumours. This is true of tropical Africa and parts of Asia: for instance, in Mozambique the incidence per 1 000 000 persons is 1038 for males and 380 for women.

Two forms of this cancer can be recognized. In one it originates in the cells of the liver substance and in the second in those lining the ducts which drain the bile from the liver. The pathologists speak of these two as hepatomas and cholangiomas. Ninety per cent of primary liver tumours are hepatomas and only 5–10 per cent are cholangiomas. In some there is a single tumour, in others the malignant changes

108

arise simultaneously in several areas.

Between 60 and 90 per cent of hepatomas develop in livers which are the seat of cirrhosis. This is a condition in which bands of intersecting scar tissue divide the organ into a collection of nodules of varying and irregular size to cause the 'hob-nail' liver. In the Western world alcohol is the best recognized cause of cirrhosis although it often arises without adequate explanation. It has been estimated that 4 per cent of persons with cirrhosis of the liver develop malignant disease of the organ. The possible role of carcinogens such as aflatoxin in Africans and Asians has been discussed in Chapter 3.

Diagnosis is difficult. In patients known to have cirrhosis of the liver sudden deterioration with rapid enlargement of the organ suggests cancerous change. In others pain under the ribs on the right side, loss of weight, perhaps jaundice, and an enlarged liver point to this diagnosis. Puncture biopsy of the liver will allow precise diagnosis and the distinction between primary and secondary cancer which can often be difficult without this evidence.

In the rare types with a single tumour removal of the part of the liver containing the cancer may be feasible. In one published series this was possible in 27.5 per cent of those in whom surgical exploration seemed justified. The death rate from operation was 12.5 per cent but 16 per cent were alive after 5 years. It has been possible in a very occasional patient to remove the whole liver and replace it by a transplanted organ. Chemotherapy has little and radiotherapy nothing to offer in this disease.

Cancer of the gall bladder

This is a rare disease in this country accounting in 1975 for 128 male deaths and 334 females with mortality rates of 5.3 and 13.2 per 1 000 000 living persons. It is associated with gall stones in 95–100 per cent of cases and, although it is generally assumed that the gall stones are responsible for it, this is by no means proved. In the women of one south-west American Indian tribe amongst whom gall stones are extremely common, cancer of the gall bladder is said to account for 25 per cent of deaths due to malignant disease. In England and Wales the figure is 0.38 per cent.

Diagnosis is difficult, but if sudden deterioration and increasing pain occur in one known to have gall stones, the possibility of cancer must be considered. In fully three-quarters of cases the growth has spread into the liver by the time of exploration and radical operation is impossible. The average survival after the impossibility of curative operation has been established is only 2½ months. Many of the patients are elderly and frail.

Because of the association of gall stones with this form of cancer, removal of any gall bladder shown to contain stones is often recommended. However, one series of 781 patients with gall stones were kept under observation without surgical treatment for 11 years and cancer developed in only 3, an incidence of 0.38 per cent. The operative mortality of cholecystectomy cannot be less than 2 per cent thus demolishing the argument for preventive removal of the gall bladder.

10

Cancer of the respiratory system

Under the head of the respiratory system are included the nasal passages and the sinuses, air-containing backwaters connected with them, the throat and larynx, the trachea or windpipe, the bronchi or air tubes within the lung, and the lung itself. Some of this territory, the nasopharynx and the pharynx, is shared with the digestive system and this common pathway, as explained in Chapter 9, sometimes called the aero-digestive tract. Cancers which originate in this area are described in the previous chapter.

Cancers of the nasal passages and the sinuses

These tumours are rare and the great majority of them arise in the sinuses: the antrum or maxillary sinus, lying within the cheek bone, is the site of about 80 per cent. In 1975 these cancers were responsible for the death of 154 men and 116 women in England and Wales, amounting to 0.22 per cent of all deaths from malignant disease. The mortality rates for that year were 6 for men and 5 for women; they have shown little change for many years. The annual registered incidence for the period 1963–6 was 9 per 1 000 000 living per year for men and 7 for women.

It is difficult to identify any constant causal factor. The geographical distribution of the disease gives no clue although it is unduly frequent in East Africa. It is also unexpectedly common in woodworkers in the furniture trade, but in them it is of unusual type being an adenocarcinoma, arising from the glands in the mucous membrane lining the sinuses, and not the common squamous variety derived from the cells of the mucous membrane itself. It is suggested that a carcinogen is present in wood dust or in some substance with which the wood has been treated. Various snuffs have been accused of responsibility, but the evidence is flimsy.

Cancer rising in the antrum extends by local spread, often into the orbit or socket of the eye, often into the nasal cavity and sometimes through the wall of the antrum to invade the skin of the cheek. Spread to the lymphatic glands is late. In the rare cases where the cancer arises in the nasal passage itself, and particularly when it lies far back, the lymphatic glands are invaded early in the disease. These tumours give rise to bleeding from one nostril and the sensation of the nasal passage on that side being blocked. There is often aching in the cheek, usually thought at first to be due to sinus infection; sometimes the pain resembles toothache. When the tumour has broken through the wall of the antrum there will be swelling of the cheek.

The diagnosis is suspected when the symptoms described become persistent. Examination will show that the affected antrum will no longer transmit light from an electric torch held in the mouth and an X-ray will also show it to be radio-opaque. The suspected antrum is punctured with a needle through the nose and the fluid withdrawn and examined for cancer cells. The final court of appeal is a surgical exploration and biopsy of any suspicious area.

The only curative treatment available at the present time is surgical removal of the tumour. The extent of the operation depends upon the extent to which the cancer has spread. It may even entail removing the contents of the eye socket. Such operations of necessity lead to considerable mutilation, although this can usually be repaired by plastic surgery. Surgery is often combined with pre-operative radiotherapy.

When the disease is too far advanced for radical operation, radiotherapy alone or sometimes in combination with chemotherapy is usually advised. Regional chemotherapy has been widely used in treating these cancers: the anticancer drug is injected through a needle inserted into the artery which supplies blood to the area bearing the tumour. The results of radiotherapy and chemotherapy alone or in combination are disappointing and offer no more than palliation.

The overall survival at 5 years is not more than 10 per

cent; when adequate surgery is possible it is between 30 and 45 per cent.

Cancer of the larynx

Cancers of the larynx or voice box are not rare. In 1975 they were recorded as causing the death of 587 men and 139 women in England and Wales, equivalent to a mortality rate of 24 and 6 per 1 000 000. They accounted for 0.6 per cent of all fatal cancers in that year. In men this tumour has shown some decrease over the past 20 years, the annual mortality rates falling from 34 (men) and 8 (women) for the quinquennium 1951–5 was to the present levels. However these figures give little indication of the true frequency of laryngeal cancer for many are cured; the registered incidence per 1 000 000 per year for the period 1963–6 was 47 for men but only 6 for women: this is undoubtedly an underestimate.

There are geographical variations in the frequency of the disease which are difficult to explain: in England it is commonest in males in the south-east, but in women much more frequently reported in the Newcastle and Leeds areas. In France the death rate for the year 1964–5 at 101 men and 11 women per 1 000 000 was between three and four times that of England and Wales.

There is little question that laryngeal cancer is associated with smoking. Because it is usually curable the association is less dramatically evident than with cancer of the lung and indeed the increase has not been of the same order. Cancer of the lung occurs more frequently in those with cancer of the larynx than in the general population.

The tumour arises from the vocal cords in about 60 per cent and usually on the most forward part; the remainder are either above or below the cords. The vocal cords are fibrous structures with scanty lymphatic vessels, consequently spread to the lymphatic glands if it arises is late. With cancers arising above and below the cords glandular invasion is often early.

When the cancer starts on one of the vocal cords the first symptom is persistent hoarseness and this is so troublesome

113

that advice is usually sought early. When the tumour is above or below the cords irritation of the throat with constant efforts to clear it and the spitting of mucous which may be blood-stained are the opening complaints, with cough and later difficulty in and pain on swallowing.

The diagnosis is made by inspecting the larynx. The surgeon is able to do this with a small mirror held at the back of the throat. More detailed examination is often required and is made through an instrument, a laryngoscope, passed down the throat under an anaesthetic. If this examination reveals a suspicious area a biopsy is made through the laryngoscope.

Treatment varies with the site of the growth and with its extent. If it is small and limited to the front part of one vocal cord with the cord itself still freely mobile, radiotherapy will cure the great majority. If it is above or below the cords or has extended to both cords, operation is normally necessary. As a rule it entails removal of the entire larynx. When lymphatic glands are enlarged their removal is undertaken at the same time. Even when they are not enlarged with tumours arising above or below the vocal cords, some surgeons prefer to remove all the lymphatic glands in the neck on the assumption that they have probably been invaded.

Rehabilitation is of the first importance after removal of the larynx, for this operation makes it impossible to produce comprehensible speech. About 60 per cent of people can be taught to speak intelligibly using the gullet to expel air, but there are some who are quite incapable of acquiring this faculty of 'oesophageal speech'. Electrical amplifying devices are available which are reasonably effective and ingenious reconstructive operations have been devised which do something to restore the voice.

The outlook in laryngeal cancer depends on its exact site of origin. When arising from the cords it is likely to be diagnosed early and when judged suitable for radiotherapy by the criteria set out above, the survival at 5 years is between 80 and 90 per cent. When it is necessary to remove the larynx the 5-year survival for all patients is 50 per cent;

if a precautionary removal of lymphatic glands from the neck is included, it rises to between 60 and 65 per cent; if the glands are not removed until they are enlarged it falls to 30 per cent. In another large series the overall survival at 5 years was 57 per cent: if the disease was localized 76 per cent, but if there were enlarged lymphatic glands 29 per cent.

Cancer of the lung

Cancer of the lung or, more accurately, cancer of the bronchus causes more deaths in England and Wales than any other form of malignant disease. In England and Wales in 1975, 32 885 persons (26 104 men and 6782 women) were certified as dying from this disease, giving mortality rates per 1 000 000 living of 1089 for men and 269 for women. These figures represent 26.9 per cent of all deaths from cancer; 39.7 per cent of all males dying from cancer and 12 per cent of all females. It is the commonest cancer causing death in men and in women second only to cancer of the breast. For every 100 women who die from lung cancer there are 385 men. Unhappily cancer of the lung is usually a lethal disease and thus the mortality figures give an accurate indication of its frequency. The registration rates of incidence in 1963–6 were 901 men and 155 women per 1 000 000 per year.

There has been a steady increase in the numbers dying from this disease over the last half-century. Changes in nomenclature have limited the comparable figures only to those since the 5-year period 1941–5. For that quinquennium the average number of men dying from this cause per year was 5292 and of women 1311: giving mortality rates of 260 and 60. Thus in this period of some 35 years the numbers dying have increased by a factor of 4.9 for men and 5.2 for women and the mortality rates by factors of 4.2 and 4.5.

In England and Wales there is an abnormally high incidence of the disease in men living in the north-west and the south-east and the London area: in women there is a striking excess in London and the south-east. Of other European countries, Finland, Holland, and Austria all report high death rates

115

from lung cancer: in Portugal the mortality rate is between one-fifth and one-sixth of that for England. In the United States 68 800 deaths from this cause were reported in 1972 making up 20 per cent of all deaths from cancer and 30 per cent of all such deaths in males.

If carcinogenic substances are present in the atmosphere it is clearly in the respiratory system that their effects will be felt. This is likely to be particularly evident in the lungs and the smaller air tubes because it is there the potential carcinogens will remain longest in contact with the cells of the lining membrane. Such substances in the atmosphere are hard to identify, but they must be presumed to exist because the incidence of lung cancer is higher in dwellers in the polluted atmosphere of towns than in those who live in the country.

There is one carcinogen the importance of which has been unshakeably established: cigarette smoke. It was in 1912 that Adler first suggested that cigarette smoking was a factor in the cause of lung cancer. In 1930 it was shown that tobacco tar painted on the skin of rabbits led to the appearance of skin cancers. It was not until 1950 that Doll and Bradford Hill proved beyond all reasonable doubt that lung cancer and cigarette smoking were related. They showed that it was twenty times more common in smokers than in non-smokers. Reports from ten different countries proved that in light smokers it was two to four times more frequent than in non-smokers, and in heavy smokers thirty-four times. It was found that those who started to smoke before the age of 15 years had a five times greater chance of dying from lung cancer than those who did not start until they were over 25. The risk decreased on giving up smoking and became progressively less as the period of abstinence lengthened. The proof is as solid as possible and room for argument no longer exists. It has been estimated that if smoking was abolished the numbers dying from lung cancer would in due time decrease by 80 per cent, or 26 000 fewer persons a year in England and Wales would die from this disease.

For many years some occupations have been known to be

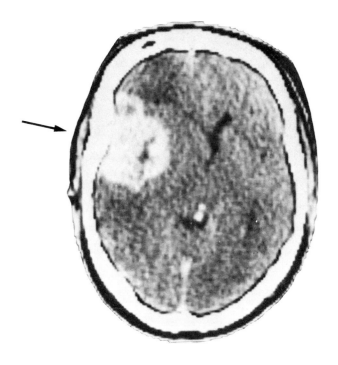

PLATE 1(*a*). Computerized axial tomographic scan of head with tumour (meningioma) showing as irregular pale area in forward half of left side.

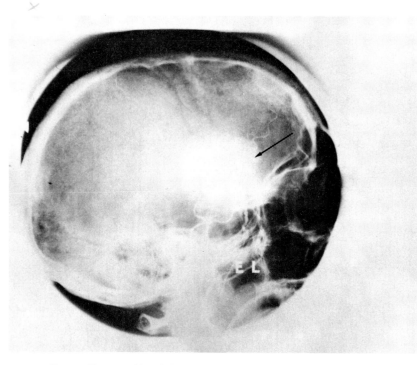

PLATE 1(*b*). X-ray film of skull of same patient as in (*a*) after injection of contrast-medium into left external carotid artery. The tumour is shown by the large opacity which vessels can be seen to enter and leave.

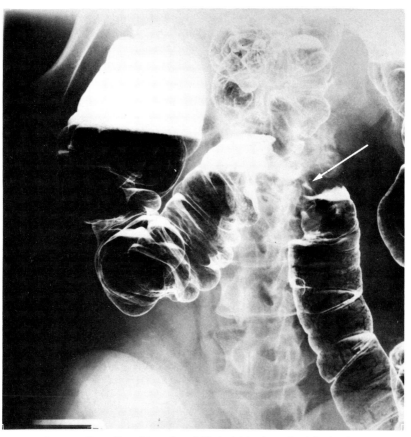

PLATE 2. X-ray film of large bowel filled with barium after injection by enema, showing a much narrowed segment due to a constricting cancer.

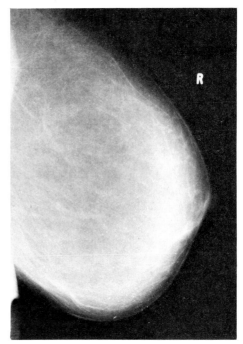

PLATE 3. Mammagram of normal right breast.

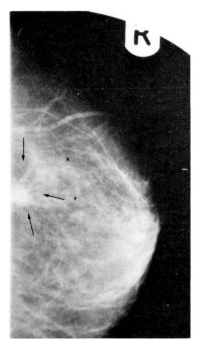

PLATE 4. Mammagram of right breast showing an irregular opacity 1 centimetre in diameter with radiating linear opacities due to a cancer which was too small to be felt with the hand.

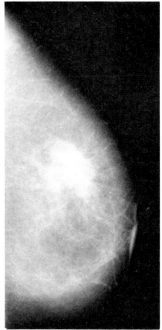

PLATE 5. Mammagram of right breast showing an irregular shadow 3 centimetres in diameter with coarse linear opacities radiating from it, due to an easily felt cancer.

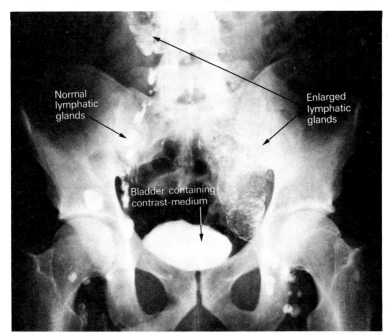

Normal lymphatic glands

Enlarged lymphatic glands

Bladder containing contrast-medium

PLATE 6. Lymphangiogram of pelvis. The bladder contains contrast-medium because an intravenous pyelogram was carried out at the same time as the lymphogram. Small normal lymphatic glands are visible in the groups in the groins. On the left side of the pelvis is a mass of enlarged glands (measuring in the original film 5 centimetres × 14 centimetres) with a foamy pattern indicating infiltration by cancer; the lower part of a similar mass can be seen on the right side alongside the spine at a higher level.

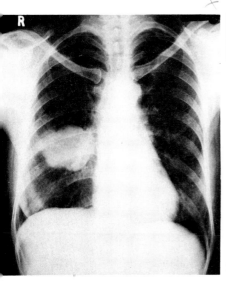

PLATE 7. X-ray film of the chest showing a large lobulated opacity in the centre of the right lung field due to cancer of the lung.

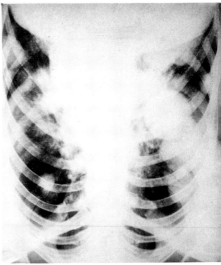

PLATE 8. X-ray film of the chest showing numerous circular opacities varying in diameter from 2 centimetres to 6 centimetres and due to 'cannon-ball' metastases from cancer of the kidney (hypernephroma).

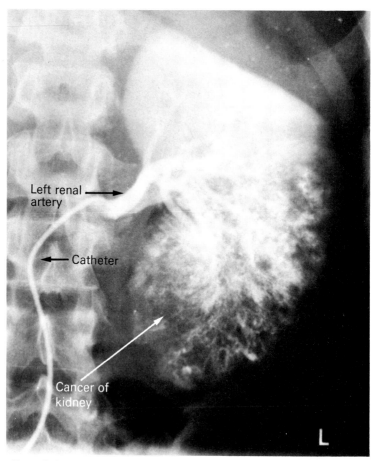

Left renal artery

Catheter

Cancer of kidney

L

PLATE 9. Arteriogram of left kidney. The catheter through which the injection of contrast-medium has been made can be seen lying in the abdominal aorta with its tip resting in the left renal artery. The arrangement of vessels in the upper third of the kidney is regular and normal, in the lower two-thirds the pattern is grossly distorted indicating a large cancer (hypernephroma) occupying this part of the organ.

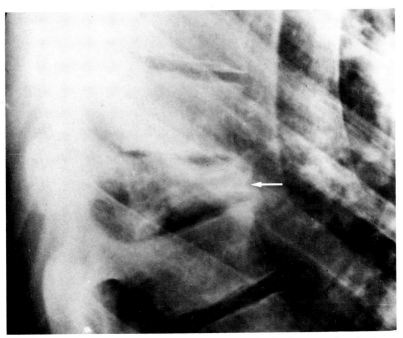

PLATE 10. X-ray film of spine showing collapse of the body of one vertebra due to a metastasis of cancer.

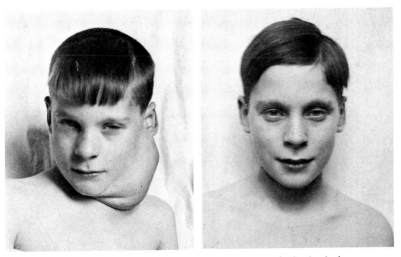

PLATE 11. Photograph showing a mass of enlarged lymphatic glands due to Hodgkin's disease in a boy of nine years (left) and his appearance after radiotherapy (right).

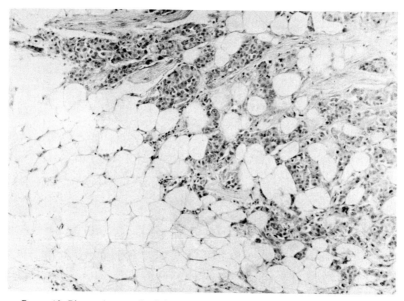

PLATE 12. Photomicrograph of the growing edge of cancer of the breast (× 130) showing the small dark cancer cells infiltrating the fatty tissue and pushing their way between the large pale fat cells.

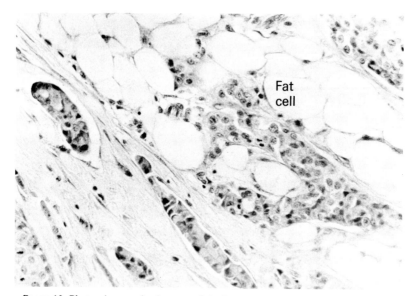

PLATE 13. Photomicrograph of cancer of the breast. The darker cancer cells can be seen thrusting forward between the normal pale fat cells and also forming columns as they permeate the lymphatic vessels (× 290).

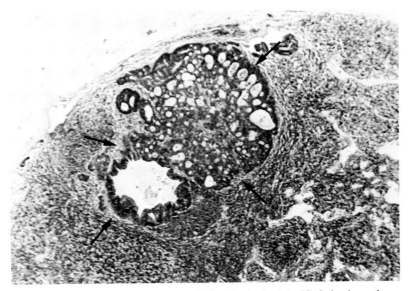

PLATE 14. Photomicrograph of part of a lymphatic gland (× 46). Lying beneath the capsule of the gland is a circumscribed area of dark-staining cells; this is a 'micro-metastasis' from a cancer of the rectum.

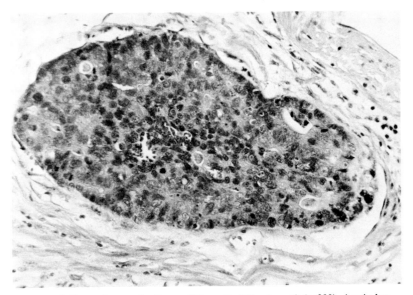

PLATE 15. Photomicrograph of part of the wall of the stomach (× 290). A vein has been cut across and can be seen to be completely filled by a mass of cancer cells which have spread from a cancer of the stomach.

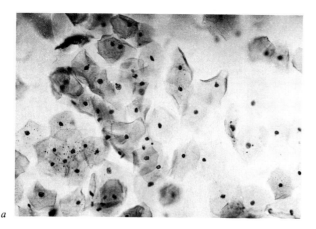

a

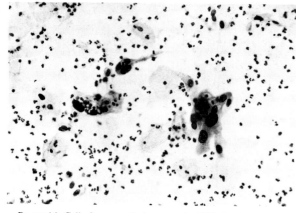

b

c

PLATE 16. Cells from cervical smears (× 280). (*a*). Normal: showing regular uniform sqamous cells from healthy cervical epithelium. (*b*). Dysphasia: a small group of four or five cells in the centre show changes which are obviously abnormal but are more or less uniform with larger nuclei having an 'open-work' pattern. (*c*). Carcinoma-in-situ: two clumps of grossly abnormal cells showing variation in size, shape, and staining qualities. These are cancer cells.

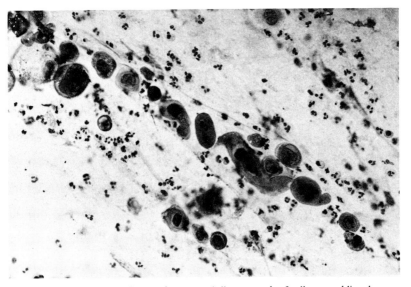

PLATE 17. Cells from tissues of sputum. A linear streak of cells runs obliquely across the field. There are large, dark staining and vary in size, shape, and the pattern of the nucleus. They are cancer cells coughed up in the phlegm of a patient with cancer of the lung (× 375).

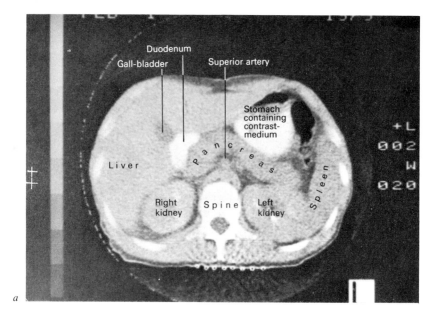

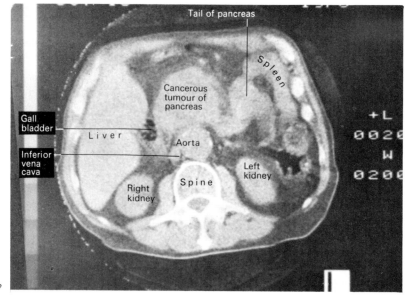

PLATE 18. Computerized axial tomographic scans of the pancreas. (*a*). Normal pancreas draped over the superior mesenteric artery with contrast-medium (gastrografin) in the stomach and descending part of the duodenum. (*b*). Pancreas with a large cancer arising from the body of the organ and lying in front of a widened aorta.

associated with an increased risk of lung cancer. As far back as 1556 the miners at St. Joachimsthal were recognized as peculiarly liable to a fatal disease they called 'Bergsucht' or mountain sickness. Only in the 1870s was this identified as cancer. Between 1869 and 1871, 10 per cent of the miners died from this cause. The Schneeberg miners were similarly affected and in 1939 it was reported that of those who died the cause in 70–80 per cent was lung cancer. The carcinogenic agent in these cases seems to have been the radioactivity of the pitchblende and other ores mined. Uranium miners in Colorado and haematite miners in the North of England are similarly at risk.

Workers with chromium compounds have also been found to have an undue liability to lung cancer and estimates have put the risk at fifteen to thirty times the normal. Breathing an atmosphere polluted with asbestos dust leads to a scarring process in the lungs called asbestosis, but only recently has it been recognized as carcinogen: characteristically it causes a rare tumour of the pleura, the membrane covering the outer surface of the lung; these tumours, known as mesotheliomas, are discussed at the end of this chapter. In workers heavily exposed to asbestos dust in textile mills the frequency of bronchial cancer is eight times that of the average, and the risk is further increased when they are also heavy smokers.

From the viewpoint of the pathologist there are several varieties of lung cancer. About 55 per cent arise from the cells which cover the mucous membrane lining the air passages, these are known as squamous carcinomas; 35 per cent arise from the cells in the deeper layer of the lining membrane and have been qualified as small cell, oat cell or undifferentiated carcinomas; about 5 per cent originate from the glands in the lining membrane and are thus adenocarcinomas. It is only the first two which are related to smoking and in smokers it is possible to recognize changes in the cells of the lining membrane which are clearly precancerous; when not advanced the appearances return to normal if smoking is discontinued.

In general terms half the tumours arise in the air tubes or

117

bronchi of the upper lobes, one-quarter in those of the lower lobes and one-quarter in the main bronchi around the root of the lung. The cancer may spread into the substance of the lung to form a local tumour; more often its grows into and blocks a bronchus so that the lung beyond the tumour becomes airless. The mucus dammed up behind the obstructing tumour provides a favourable soil for the growth of bacteria and thus becomes the seat of infection. The cancer, especially when it arises near the root of the lung, spreads early to the local lymphatic glands. Those at the lung root are first invaded; then those in the mediastinum, the area between the two lungs; those alongside the windpipe; and often those at the root of the neck. Sometimes the bronchi are invaded by a sheet of cancer cells growing along the lymphatic vessels. Spread to the lymphatic glands is present in 50 per cent of all patients when they first seek advice and when the cancer is of the small cell type the proportion rises to 80 per cent. Distant blood-borne metastases are often early and are particularly common in the liver, brain, and bone: they are earlier and more common with adenocarcinoma than with the other two varieties.

The symptoms of lung cancer depend largely upon its site of origin. About 5 per cent are found by chance in a routine X-ray examination of the chest. In 10 per cent the first complaints are seemingly unconnected with the lungs: they either arise from a secondary deposit, such as a metastasis in the brain, or as the result of an endocrine or neurological disturbance of the type described in Chapter 4. These strange complications are more common with lung cancer than with any other type of malignant disease. Of the 85 per cent that remain the symptoms are those of chest disease: cough, spitting of blood, and breathlessness are all common. Sometimes an attack of what appears to be pneumonia is the opening event and only when the anticipated recovery does not take place is the true cause appreciated. Sometimes the patient is aware of a constant and localized wheeze within the chest. Pain may, like that of pleurisy, come and go with

the movements of breathing; sometimes there is a deep
central boring sensation due to enlarged lymphatic glands.
on occasions a cancer at the upper extremity of the lung will
spread to invade ribs and nerves with pain in the shoulder
and arm. Local extension to the surface of the lung will
lead to the accumulation of fluid in the chest. Sometimes
spread to the membrane around the heart, the pericardium,
causes fluid to form in this situation.

It will be seen that the patterns of illness which lung
cancer may cause are varied and often diagnostically misleading: nevertheless when cough, phlegm, and spitting of
blood make a sudden appearance in a middle-aged smoker
this disease is likely to be the cause.

Diagnosis seldom offers great difficulty. An X-ray of the
chest may show a shadow which arouses suspicions of cancer.
To establish the diagnosis requires the identification of cancer cells: these may be found in the phlegm coughed up, but
this is a test which demands considerable experience of
cytology. If fluid has accumulated around the lung, cancer
cells may be found in a specimen drawn off by syringe. In
many, if not most, patients it is necessary to pass an instrument, a bronchoscope, down the windpipe. Through it the
tumour can usually be seen and a piece of tissue removed
for microscopic examination. Biopsy of an enlarged gland,
felt in the neck, will often provide the proof required. Often
the X-ray films show glands to be enlarged in the mediastinum,
the central area between the two lungs: it is then possible to
carry out mediastinoscopy, making a small incision in the
neck through which an endoscope may be passed and a gland
removed. Even when all these methods are available in
perhaps one-fifth of patients an exploratory operation on
the lung is necessary.

Surgical operation for complete removal of the tumour
offers virtually the only chance of cure. It is often difficult
to be certain whether this is feasible without preliminary
exploration, but in many cases it is only too easy to decide
that it is impossible and that exploration is not justifiable.

Cancer – the facts

The points which need to be decided before an exploratory operation is undertaken are three: whether there are distant secondary deposits or extensive spread to glands within the chest; whether the tumour has extended locally to invade neighbouring organs so as to make removal impossible; and whether the patient's general health is sufficiently good and his breathing machinery adequate to withstand a formidable operation which will result in a considerable reduction in respiratory efficiency. The second of these may be a difficult decision and exploratory operation will often show that complete removal is not possible. In one large series of over 5000 patients with lung cancer no surgical exploration was considered justified in 70 per cent. In 37 per cent there were distant metastases; in 11 per cent local spread was considered to make removal impossible; in 5 per cent the general health was so poor and in 17 per cent the efficiency of the lungs so impaired that operation was judged to be unwarranted. Of the 30 per cent in whom operation was undertaken, a radical removal was carried out in two-thirds. Thus of over 5000 patients, 'curative' surgery was possible in only 1092 or one-fifth. Such figures, it must be stressed, are not truly representative because a proportion of patients with lung cancer are so ill that they are not referred to hospital. Of the totality of sufferers, therefore, well under one-fifth are suitable for curative surgery when they first seek advice.

The operation the surgeon carries out is either removal of one lung or of a lobe of one lung. Opinion has swung in favour of the second and lesser procedure when this is possible, but both carry a considerable immediate risk. The operative mortality, a term which may be defined as the percentage of patients undergoing surgery who die before discharge from hospital, was 9 per cent for removal of a single lobe (lobectomy) and 17 per cent for removal of an entire lung (pneumonectomy). In one large series reported a lobectomy was possible in one quarter and pneumonectomy was required in the remainder. The results of surgery judged the numbers of survivors after 5 years are remarkably similar from all centres and have changed little over the past 10–15 years: the figure is constantly in the region of 25 per cent.

Radiotherapy has been used extensively in the treatment of lung cancer. As a primary radical treatment its value is limited. A careful comparison has been made between the results of operation and those of radiotherapy in the treatment of the particular type of lung cancer described as 'oat cell' carcinoma. The results of surgery in this variety are unfavourable and contrast strongly with those in the squamous form. After 21 months only 4 per cent of those operated upon survived, while 10 per cent receiving radiotherapy were still living. The results of neither treatment are encouraging but radiotherapy has a clear advantage in this type of lung cancer. Moreover at the time when this trial was carried out the dose of irradiation was considerably smaller than that usual today and the proportion cured by radiotherapy would probably now be greater than 10 per cent.

Pre-operative irradiation has been widely used, but in general has not been shown to increase the number surviving. There is one situation in which it is useful: in some cancers which arise at the extreme apex of the lung local extension occurs with invasion of the ribs and the nerves in the neighbourhood causing pain in the arm and shoulder. Radical operation is sometimes made possible in such patients by preliminary radiotherapy. Post-operative radiotherapy does not improve the survival rate. It does decrease the number of local recurrences of the tumour, but appears to increase the frequency of distant metastases.

When curative surgery is impossible radiotherapy is often prescribed. A trial was made in which the survival of untreated patients with inoperable tumours was compared with that of similar patients receiving 'radical' radiotherapy. This term indicates a dosage of irradiation which theoretically should cure the cancer. One-half of those treated were dead in 4½ months and one-half of those untreated in 3½ months. At the end of a year 18 per cent of the treated and 14 per cent of the untreated survived. The conclusion to be drawn from these figures is that radiotherapy is not justified in inoperable lung cancer unless there is some specific symptom, either local or due to metastases, it may relieve. In such circumstances it should be given in 'palliative' and not 'curative' doses.

Chemotherapy has been disappointing. It can lead to reduction in the size of the tumour and the 'oat cell' variety is more sensitive than the squamous type. In inoperable cases it seldom prolongs survival by more than two or three weeks, although occasionally a dramatic improvement occurs particularly when symptoms are due to a secondary deposit, for instance, in the brain. It has been used post-operatively and a claim has been made that in the 'oat cell' type of cancer it prolonged the proportion surviving after 4 years from 4 per cent to 16 per cent.

Recently Japanese workers have claimed a notable improvement with intermittent chemotherapy combined with surgery. They used two anticancer drugs which are not easily obtainable outside Japan. These were given together in courses lasting a month. The first course was given one-half before and one-half immediately after operation, subsequent courses followed at intervals of 3 months during the first year after operation and at intervals of 6 months for the second and third years. The results have been compared with those of a group of patients who had undergone radical surgery alone. In the group without chemotherapy 22.6 per cent were alive after 5 years. In those who had undergone surgery and had had one course of chemotherapy 23 per cent survived 5 years; of those who had had two courses the proportion surviving was 29.3 per cent and having had three or more courses 50.9 per cent. These results have been criticized because the group receiving no chemotherapy was not treated at the same time as those receiving it, making comparison unsafe. Nevertheless these remarkable figures, if they can be confirmed, represent double the rate of cure obtained by surgery alone.

Cancers of the respiratory system

In spite of this the outlook of this, the cancer responsible for more than a quarter of all deaths from malignant disease, remains depressing. In less than one-fifth of those presenting for treatment is radical surgery feasible and of those who survive operation three-quarters will be dead within 5 years. Earlier diagnosis, although clearly desirable, is hard to achieve. Regular X-rays of the chest in those at risk might well increase the proportion in which radical surgery was possible. To all it is clear that the essential preventive measure is an interdiction on the smoking of cigarettes. It is estimated that this would eventually decrease the numbers dying of lung cancer in England and Wales by 26 000 a year. Clearly to abolish cigarette smoking by legislation would not be acceptable. Attempts to educate the public and to discourage the habit in young people have been unavailing. The social and commercial implications of the problem appear insuperable and the fact that the tax on tobacco in 1974–5 contributed £1 337 400 000 to the national revenue or 5.7 per cent of the total makes restrictive measures no easier.

Cancer of the pleura

The mesothelioma, a rare malignant tumour of the pleura, the membrane covering the surface of the lung, has been recognized for many years. It has been reported increasingly often of late years and there is no doubt that it is usually related to exposure to asbestos dust. Inhalation of this dust leads to a generalized scarring of the lungs which may prove fatal and which may be associated with this cancerous change in the covering pleural membrane. Men are affected more often than women and the period between exposure to the dust and the appearance of the tumour is said to average 37 years. This form of cancer causes fluid to form between the layer of pleura which covers the lung and that which lines the inner surface of the chest wall. Diagnosis is often difficult. The history of exposure to asbestos usually provides the clue and fibres of asbestos, 'asbestos bodies', are often found on examination of the phlegm. Treatment is usually unavailing, but the disease is only slowly progressive.

123

11

Cancer of the urinary system

The urinary system includes the kidneys (which act as filters removing waste products, excess water and other substances from the blood), the ureters, the urinary bladder, the urethra, and the prostate. The ureters, the channels which carry the urine from the kidneys to the bladder, each widens to a funnel shape at its upper end, known as the pelvis, where it is attached to the kidney. The urethra is the passage which carries the urine from the bladder to the exterior and at the neck of the bladder in the male it traverses a gland known as the prostate.

Cancers of the kidney

Malignant disease of the kidney is uncommon. In 1975 it was the certified cause of death of 974 men and 598 women in England and Wales. The mortality rates per 1 000 000 living were 41 for men and 24 for women. It formed 1.5 per cent of all fatal cancers in men and 1.1 per cent in women.

There are two important forms of cancer of the kidney and a number of other rare varieties. The first which is much the most frequent is seen in adults and, in pathological terms, is a carcinoma, arising from the cells of the substance of the organ. It was formerly called a hypernephroma or sometimes a Grawitz tumour after the man who first described it. The second, which occurs in children, is the nephroblastoma arising from cells which appear to have been left behind during the development of the kidney in the unborn child.

The cause of the carcinoma of the kidney is unknown. In some animals tumours of the kidney are due to infection by viruses but there is nothing to suggest that this may be true of man. It has been found that Syrian hamsters develop cancer of the kidney if dosed with large quantities of oestrogen,

124

Cancer of the urinary system

one of the female sex hormones. However, there is no evidence that hormones are important in this connection in man, but the observation has encouraged the treatment of this type of malignant disease with hormones antagonistic to oestrogen. It is debatable whether detectable benefit ensues.

The cancer arises from the cells of the tubules of the kidney and its mode of spread is unusual for it often rapidly invades the veins. Blood-borne metastases in the lungs, bone and brain are thus likely to occur early and often precede spread to the lymphatic glands of the region.

The commonest initial symptom is the passage of blood-stained urine. Pain may be entirely absent, but there is sometimes complaint of aching in the loin. On occasion a metastasis will cause the first symptom, at other times cancer of the kidney gives rise to a feverish illness which may baffle the doctor.

The diagnosis depends upon physical examination which may disclose an obvious enlargement of one kidney, but further tests are required to establish the nature of the swelling. If no tumour can be felt, diagnosis rests entirely upon instrumental investigation. It is usual to pass a cysto-scope, an instrument through which the interior of the bladder may be inspected: this will reveal whether the bleeding is coming from the kidney and if so from which one. Radiological examination after intravenous injection of a dye excreted by the kidney and opaque to X-rays will reveal enlargement or deformity of the organ. Sometimes X-ray films are taken after injection of radio-opaque agents into the artery to the kidney to outline and define the tumour (see Plate 9). Cancer of the kidney often has to be distinguished from a cyst and this can be done by puncturing the swelling with a needle and drawing off fluid with a syringe. This method is not conclusive for in some 6 per cent of cases a cancer will cause a cyst to form.

Removal of the kidney affected by cancer is the accepted treatment of this disease. Of recent years it has been shown that it is sometimes possible to remove the tumour and conserve much of the kidney. Pre-operative radiotherapy may make it possible to operate when the growth has spread outside the kidney, but in general it is a tumour which is not normally sensitive to irradiation.

It is recognized as a form of cancer liable to behave in an unexpected fashion. It has been noted to regress spontaneously and metastases sometimes remit without treatment. Solitary metastases are not rare and it is often justifiable to excise them when the primary cancer has apparently been cured.

The generalized stage is difficult to treat. Radiotherapy may relieve pain from metastases in bones but has little value otherwise; the results of chemotherapy are disappointing. A synthetic hormone-like drug, medroxyprogesterone, has been recommended in man with generalized disease; its effects are unconvincing.

The overall survival for 5 years is 20 per cent. When the kidney is not fixed to the surrounding tissues and there are no metastases 50 per cent are living 5 years after treatment.

The nephroblastoma is a rare cancer of the kidney which arises from the primitive cells from which the kidney is formed in foetal life and which have normally disappeared by birth. Most cases are seen in children between the ages of 3 and 4 years; boys are more often affected than girls and in 5–10 per cent tumours are found in both kidneys. Its importance is out of proportion to its frequency because it is one of the cancers in which chemotherapy has established its value.

Nephroblastoma makes up about 12 per cent of childhood cancers. It gives rise early to metastases and these may be the cause of the first symptom. More often the mother notices that her child's abdomen is swelling and that there is progressive loss of flesh. It rarely causes bleeding into the urine.

It is one of the diseases in which co-operation between surgeon, radiotherapist, and oncologist is important. The basic treatment consists of removal of the kidney and the cancer it carries: pre-operative radiotherapy will often shrink the tumour sufficiently to make this possible and post-operative radiotherapy will increase the 5-year survival from 30 per cent to 50 per cent. Repeated courses of chemotherapy, using the drug Actinomycin D, have increased the survival at 5 years to 80 per cent after satisfactory removal of the primary cancer. If this drug is given for 5 months after operation the incidence of metastases is reduced from 50 per cent to 20 per cent.

Cancer of the bladder and ureter

The urine is made by the kidney from which it is drained through the pelvis of the kidney, into the ureters which carry it to the bladder. The lining membrane or epithelium which covers the inner surface of all these behaves similarly. Cancer may arise from its cells in any of these areas, although it is far more common in the bladder than elsewhere. The following paragraphs concern themselves only with cancer of the bladder unless otherwise noted.

In 1975, 2837 men and 1227 women in England and Wales were certified as dying from cancer of the bladder; the figures for cancer of the pelvis of the kidney were 38 and 16 and for cancer of the ureter 37 and 24. The mortality rates for cancer of the bladder in 1975 were 118 for men and 49 for women. There has been a steady rise in this rate for this type of cancer to these figures; thus for the quinquennium 1951-5 they were 85 for men and 35 for women per year. Cancer of the bladder is two or three times commoner in men than in women and accounts for 3.3 per cent of those dying from malignant disease.

It can be readily understood that chemical carcinogens might be expected to cause cancer of the bladder. These substances once they enter the body are likely to be removed by the filtering action of the kidney and excreted in the urine which constantly bathes the epithelium lining the ureters, but remains for a much longer period in contact with that of the bladder.

As long ago as 1894 the undue frequency of this disease in workers in the aniline dye industry was noted. It was thought for many years that aniline itself was the carcinogen and only later recognized that a by-product of dye manufacture, 2-naphthylamine, was the agent responsible. It or related substances have been found responsible for the increased risk of cancer of the bladder in the chemical industry as well as those concerned with rubber and the making of cables. There is evidence too that smoking increases the risk of developing this disease. It is said that the period of exposure before cancer is likely to appear is 30 years and because that needed to induce cancer of the lung is only 20 years, many have perished of the second before the first could become manifest.

The common benign warty growths of the bladder lining – the papilloma – are frequently a precancerous disorder. Another frequent association is with a parasite schistosoma, which invades the wall of the bladder. Its presence causes chronic irritation which may be followed by cancer. This infection, carried in the water of the Nile, explains why cancer of the bladder is probably the commonest variety of malignant disease in Egypt.

Cancers of the bladder vary greatly in their degree of malignancy, some remain confined to the mucous membrane for a long while; others, rapidly invasive, spread through the bladder wall into the pelvic tissues and the lymphatic glands of the region and lead to early metastasis in the lung and the liver.

The initial symptom of cancer of the bladder is almost constantly the presence of blood in the urine. It is unassociated with pain or other abnormality of the bladder's function. Sometimes the complaint is of having to pass water unduly often and of burning pain while doing so, the symptoms of cystitis.

There are seldom any signs of disease to be found on physical examination. It may be possible to identify cancer cells in the urine and a search for them is sometimes used as a screening test for those in occupations which carry an increased risk of this disease. The essential examination is

Cancer of the urinary system

inspection of the interior of the bladder through a cystoscope. The source of bleeding can be identified and, if a cancer or a suspicious area is seen, a biopsy can be made. If the symptoms are those of cystitis, but the laboratory is unable to cultivate bacteria from the urine, a likely explanation is cancer and investigation is advisable.

The appropriate treatment for cancer of the bladder depends upon the character of the tumour and its position. The choice is between radiotherapy and surgery. Non-invasive cancers can be cured by destruction by heat (diathermy) with or without removal through a cystoscope. An infiltrating cancer of the upper part of the bladder can be removed surgically. When the base of the bladder is the seat of the tumour and when there is invasion of its floor the choice lies between removal of the entire bladder, perhaps with implantation of the ureters into the large bowel, and radiotherapy. It is an operation making great demands on both patient and surgeon and the results of radiotherapy are but little different. Pre-operative radiotherapy will sometimes allow surgery which at first seemed technically impossible. Chemotherapy has at present little to offer.

The outlook in cancer of the bladder depends upon the position of the tumour and its degree of malignancy. The overall 5-year survival is about 37 per cent, but where there is no more than slight invasion of the wall of the bladder it rises to 44 per cent. With small and entirely superficial cancers, 60–80 per cent of those treated are alive after 5 years; on the other hand, when the growth is at the base of the bladder and infiltrating deeply into its wall, not more than 15 per cent are likely to live as long as this.

Cancer of the prostate
The prostate is a gland lying at the base of the bladder in men. It encircles the urethra, the channel through which the bladder empties and urine is passed. It often becomes enlarged with advancing years and in 10 per cent of elderly men the enlargement is sufficient to cause troublesome symptoms.

It is also often the seat of malignant disease and although benign enlargement is frequently associated it does not appear to be the cause of the cancer. It is not always easy to define cancer of the prostate for it may remain latent. Often when the gland is removed because its enlargement was interfering with the bladder's emptying, microscopic examination will unexpectedly show a minute area of cancerous change. Operation in such cases is seldom followed by recurrence. It is impossible to say whether the malignant disease would eventually have declared itself or whether it would have remained permanently silent. With the increasing number of operations for removal of the enlarged prostate, the finding of this latent cancer is more and more common.

In 1975, 4421 men were certified as dying of cancer of the prostate, a number amounting to 6.7 per cent of all male deaths from malignant disease. The mortality rate per 1 000 000 living men was 184. This form of cancer is preponderantly a disease of the elderly: thus in 1975 the mortality rate was 19 for men aged 45–54 years and 4512 for those above the age of 85 years. It has become increasingly common as a certified cause of death in the last half-century: the mortality rate per 1 000 000 living per year was only 25 for the quinquennium 1911–15 but for 1966–70 it was 168, more than a five-fold increase. Much of this is due to the increasing longevity of the population and some probably to the discovery of latent cancers previously unrecognized.

By the pathologist the cancer is described as an adenocarcinoma for it arises from the glandular cells in the prostate. There is great variation in the degree of malignancy of these tumours: at one end of the scale is the latent variety previously mentioned, at the other a growth which rapidly invades the bladder and spreads quickly to the lymphatic glands in the vicinity. Cancer of the prostate has a striking tendency to cause metastases in bone, and particularly in the vertebrae to which it probably spreads from the lymphatic glands alongside the spine. Secondary deposits in the skeleton have been reported in over 80 per cent of those in

Cancer of the urinary system

whom the disease has become generalized. They usually cause increased density of the bone and only rarely a pathological feature.

In four out of five men with cancer of the prostate the initial symptoms are not to be distinguished from those due to a benign enlargement of the gland. They consist of a desire to pass water more frequently, particularly at night, slowness in starting the act and a weak stream. The symptoms advance more rapidly when a cancer is the cause of prostatic enlargement than when it is benign. In about 12 per cent the urine is intermittently blood-stained and in another 12 per cent the early symptoms are due to metastases. These may be pain in the bones, particularly backache, or sometimes anaemia resulting from the cancer spreading through the bone-marrow and destroying the tissues which form the blood cells.

The diagnosis is usually made by physical examination. The prostate can be felt by a finger introduced into the rectum and a cancer can often be recognized by an irregular, craggy enlargement of the gland. In other instances rectal examination may be inconclusive. A laboratory test often of the greatest value is an estimation of a substance in the blood called the acid phosphatase. This is a secretion of the glandular cells of the prostate and when there is a malignant overgrowth of the cells the quantity of acid phosphates in the blood may be greatly increased. This increase is particularly marked when there are extensive metastases and when the cancer cells are not so abnormal that they have lost the functions of their tissue of origin. Ultimate proof of the diagnosis is given, as in all malignant disease, by microscopic study of material from the gland obtained either by needle puncture or through a cystoscope passed into the bladder.

X-ray films will often show increased density of the bones due to metastases and puncture of the bone-marrow may yield cancer cells.

If microscopic cancer is found unexpectedly in an operation specimen, further treatment is not required. When firm diagnosis is established the therapeutic choices often are surgery, treatment with hormones, and radiotherapy. Which of these is selected depends upon the extent of the growth and to a lesser extent upon the patient's age and general health. Radical surgical removal of the gland is seldom practised in the United Kingdom. It would be justifiable in a healthy man aged 50 to 60 years where the tumour was still confined to the gland. More commonly surgery is limited to operations carried out through a cystoscope to relieve obstruction to the outflow of urine.

Cancer of the prostate is greatly influenced by treatment with female sex hormones called oestrogens. These are prescribed, usually as stilboestrol, a synthetic preparation with oestrogen-like activity, when surgery is inadvisable. The effects are often rapid and dramatic: symptoms due to metastases disappear, the tumour shrinks, bladder troubles resolve and health is greatly improved. This is remission, but not cure; after a period which may exceed 5 years the response fails and the cancer escapes from control. At this stage castration may be followed by further remission.

Radiotherapy is used rather more than it was a few years ago. Supervoltage techniques have proved capable of controlling cancer of the prostate at all stages. It is not applicable to diffuse metastases in bone, for it would cause irreversible damage to the bone-marrow, but it will often cause the local tumour of the gland to shrink and may relieve obstruction to the passage of urine.

Overall some 38 per cent of men with cancer of the prostate will be alive 5 years after the diagnosis is made. Of those where the disease is still confined to the gland itself when first treated the survival at 5 years is 53 per cent.

12

Cancer of the breast

Cancer of the breast is responsible for more women dying than any other malignant disease. In England and Wales in 1975, 11 637 deaths were certified as due to this cause: it accounted for 20.5 per cent of all deaths in women due to cancer. The mortality rate for this year was 461 per 1 000 000 living and it has shown a steady increase over the last 60 years. For the quinquennium 1911–15 it was 198, by 1966–70 it had risen to 415, and the rise still continues. Cancer of the breast becomes increasingly common with advancing years: in 1975 the age-adjusted mortality rate per 1 000 000 living women aged 35–44 years was 256, but for those aged 75–84 it was 1582. Thus the increasing longevity of the population accounts for some of the overall increase, but it seems unlikely that it is sufficient to explain it all. In men cancer of the breast is a rare disease causing only 82 deaths in 1975 with a mortality rate of 3.

This disease is commoner than the mortality figures indicate. The inaccuracy of figures for incidence has been discussed earlier: in general, they tend to be lower than true levels. Nevertheless for the years 1963–6 659 women per 1 000 000 per year were registered as suffering from cancer of the breast compared with a mortality rate of 394 per 1 000 000 per year for the same period. This difference agrees roughly with the overall 'cure' rate of about 45 per cent.

Cancer of the breast is as common in the United States, Canada, and the European countries as it is in the United Kingdom. It is rare in the Far East, particularly in Japan, where the mortality rate is between 30 and 40 per 1 000 000 living. It is uncommon too in Venezuela and other Latin American countries.

Cancer – the facts

In 1932 it was shown that a virus played a part in the cause of cancer of the mammary glands in mice. The effect of this agent, which became known as the Bittner factor, was modified by other influences such as the breed of mouse and the activity of the animals' endocrine glands. This discovery naturally raised the possibility of a virus being of importance in human breast cancer and interest was rekindled when in 1970 a virus capable of being propagated outside the body was recovered from a cancer of the breast in a monkey. Within the last few years a virus with some resemblance to the Bittner factor has been found in 6 per cent of normal women and in more than 25 per cent of women with cancer of the breast. Although these observations must be regarded as suggestive, there is no firm proof that a virus plays an important role, or indeed any role, in the cause of the human disease.

The cause of cancer of the breast, like that of other cancers, remains a mystery, but a number of factors appear to have some influence. The disease is less common in women whose first pregnancy occurs before they reach the age of 20; in those who bear many children; in those whose ovaries are removed before the age of 37; in the lower socio-economic groups; and in those of non-Caucasian race. It occurs less commonly in societies where breast-feeding is the rule. This physiological activity is becoming increasingly rare in the Western nations. In the United States in 1920, 70 per cent of mothers breast-fed their children, in 1974 the proportion was less than 18 per cent.

By contrast a number of factors can be recognized which increase the risk of developing cancer of the breast. It is three to five times more common in blood relatives of those affected and, when the daughter of a woman with this disease develops cancer of the breast, it tends to appear at an age 10 years younger than in her mother. The common cystic disease of the breast – formerly called chronic mastitis – increases the risk of cancer by two to three times and even more if it is treated with male sex hormones (androgens).

Cancer of the breast

Mastitis has in the past been treated by radiotherapy and this further increases the risk. Women who have been cured of cancer of the breast have a 10–20 per cent chance of developing a second tumour within 20 years.

The cancer almost always arises from the cells lining the ducts in the breast and in 1–2 per cent tumours are to be found in both breasts when the patient first consults her doctor. If neglected it extends locally becoming fixed to the muscles beneath the breast and if it arises near the surface it may become attached to the skin. It spreads to the lymphatic glands in the armpit of the same side and later to those near the collar bone and deep to the breast within the chest. Distant secondary deposits are common and in those who have died of the disease are particularly frequent in the lungs, the liver, the bones, and the skin. It seems likely that they are spread through the blood stream from the diseased lymphatic glands, because the more numerous the glands affected the more extensive the metastases.

One of the mysterious features of cancer of the breast is the long period for which the disease may remain dormant. There is a close relationship between the size of the cancer when it is first treated, the frequency of metastases, and the lapse of time before they make their appearance. When the tumour only measures one centimetre in diameter metastases eventually develop in 27 per cent after an interval averaging 10 years. When the tumour measures six centimetres the proportion rises to 58 per cent. The average period for all tumours before the appearance of metastases is 4 years.

Four out of five women with cancer of the breast consult their doctors with symptoms suggesting breast disease. Commonly a lump in the breast has been noticed: sometimes the nipple is seen to be drawn in; there is swelling of the skin; or rarely a little bleeding from the nipple. In the other fifth the trouble is found at a routine examination for some other purpose or on screening. Rarely a metastasis causes the initial symptoms. When a swelling is felt it is characteristically hard, with ill-defined outlines and sometimes fixed to the muscles on the wall of the chest or to the skin over the breast. Occasionally the first sign is a condition of the nipple resembling eczema and known as Paget's disease, and more rarely the tumour advances so rapidly that the breast appears inflamed. When advice is first sought the tumour in the breast averages three to four centimetres in diameter and in 45 per cent enlarged lymphatic glands are to be felt in the armpit. In perhaps 1 woman in a 100 tumours are found in both breasts.

There is not usually great difficulty in distinguishing a cancer from other diseases of the breast. There is a common benign tumour called a fibroadenoma, which has well-defined characteristics. The other two disorders which may be misleading are the cystic disease already mentioned and localized thickening, often resulting from injury, called 'fat necrosis'. Mammography and thermography may reinforce suspicions. They are described in the chapter on screening. The presence of a cyst can be confirmed by puncturing it with a needle and drawing off the fluid it contains. Nevertheless the only way of being certain is by biopsy and microscopic study of the diseased tissue and this is essential if there is any doubt. It may be safe to wait and watch developments in a woman under 35 years of age, but in those older delay carries an unacceptable risk.

Once the diagnosis has been confirmed, rational treatment can be planned only when the distribution of the disease has been defined. Physical examination will show if the lymphatic glands under the arm and in other groups are enlarged; nodules in the skin and notable enlargement of the liver can be detected. X-ray films of the lungs may show metastases. Laboratory tests of the liver may indicate that secondary deposits have interfered with its normal functioning. X-rays and isotopic scans of the skeleton may reveal metastases in the bones. In spite of all these sophisticated investigations many metastases elude detection. Many deposits in bone escape notice and the liver is affected at least twice as often as tests suggest.

Although cancer of the breast is one of the commonest of

Cancer of the breast

all malignant diseases and many centres throughout the world have a massive experience of the condition, there is little agreement on the details of primary treatment. When disease is limited to the breast with no enlargement of lymphatic glands or only of those in the armpit, most would agree that the tumour should be removed. The operations recommended range from what is called radical mastectomy to simple excision of that part of the breast containing the tumour. The first entails removal of the whole breast, the overlying skin, the underlying muscles, and the lymphatic glands in the armpit. Lesser operations include simple removal of the whole breast (simple mastectomy) with or without removal of the lymphatic glands. The general trend is for the surgical approach to be more conservative. In many countries surgery is followed by radiotherapy to the area of the breast and armpit. Claims have been made that when there are no enlarged lymphatic glands there is no difference between the results of radical mastectomy, simple mastectomy followed by radiotherapy, and simple mastectomy with removal of the lymphatic glands in the armpit. When these glands are enlarged radical mastectomy is said to give the same results as simple mastectomy followed by radiotherapy. The fact that there is no agreement on the best surgical approach to this problem 90 years after Halstead first described the operation of radical mastectomy suggests that the extent of the operation matters little provided the tumour is removed. If this is so there is justification for recommending a conservative measure such as simple mastectomy followed by radiotherapy. It is as yet uncertain whether removal of only that part of the breast containing the tumour gives results comparable with those of simple mastectomy. It has been claimed that local mastectomy with careful follow-up and radiotherapy only when indicated by developments gives results as good as those of preventive radiotherapy immediately after operation.

Recently post-operative chemotherapy has been recommended for those with enlarged lymphatic glands. It has taken the form of repeated courses of drugs in combination and appears to prolong the interval before recurrence takes place. In one series given monthly courses of chemotherapy for a year after mastectomy only 2 per cent had relapsed after 2 years whereas in those who received no chemotherapy the relapse rate was 12 per cent.

It has been suggested that at the time of the primary operation, the opposite breast should also be removed as a preventive measure. Only 6 per cent of women with cancer of the breast develop another primary tumour in the second breast and 80 per cent of these occur within 5 years of the first. Careful supervision for 5 years is all that is required.

If distant metastases are present when the patient is first seen or when recurrence has taken place, the indications for treatment are different. Local recurrences in the area of the primary tumour, in the chest wall or in the lymphatic glands of the region respond well to radiotherapy. This will permanently control at least 60 per cent and it is also valuable in the treatment of secondary deposits in bones, being particularly effective in the relief of pain.

Disseminated cancer of the breast is one of the malignant diseases which partly depends for its growth on hormonal influences and in this stage can often be greatly helped by alteration in the balance of hormones. It has been known for years that removal of the ovaries in women with cancer of the breast before the change of life will often bring much benefit and in 20–40 per cent this improvement is striking, although seldom lasting more than a year. Treatment with hormones is also often effective. The preparations most often used are male sex hormones (androgens), female sex hormones (oestrogens), and cortisone-like drugs (corticosteroids). Before the menopause and for 5 years afterwards androgens are likely to be most effective; for 6–10 years after there is little to choose between the effects of androgens and oestrogens; and more than 10 years after the change of life, oestrogens are more active. Metastases in the lung, the skin, and the tissues just below the skin respond best; the effects upon those in the liver and the brain are slight; and those in bone occupy an intermediate position. The results of treatment may be classed as excellent in 25 per cent of those receiving androgens, 34 per cent of those having oestrogens, and 21 per cent with corticosteroids. The last may be combined with either of the other two and its effect is not dependant upon its relation to the menopause. Improvement averages 18–24 months in duration.

Surgical operations to alter the balance of the endocrine glands are undertaken only when the treatment with hormones has failed. The exception to this is removal of the ovaries which is usually the first step in women who have not reached the menopause. The operations carried out are removal of the adrenal glands or removal of the pituitary gland. The effects of the two are much the same and tend to be better in those who have shown improvement after removal of the ovaries. Worthwhile improvement is seen in 30–60 per cent of those undergoing one or other of these operations and lasts an average of 18–24 months. The mortality of the operations is about 5 per cent.

Chemotherapy has been widely used in disseminated cancer of the breast. At first single drugs were used, but now successive courses of combinations of agents are the rule. Improvement is seen in 50–80 per cent. In some series reported all signs of disease have disappeared in half the patients treated, but relapse at present seems inevitable and the average duration of the improvement is only 4–12 months. Trials of different combinations of drugs are in progress throughout the world and the results although at present unimpressive do give some hope for the future.

If cancer of the breast is untreated 20 per cent of women survive 5 years but at 10 years less than 10 per cent are still alive. The length of survival depends so much on the size of the tumour when treatment was started that overall figures have little meaning, but the proportion of untreated patients surviving at 5 years of untreated patients is 44 per cent. If only patients with Stage I or II disease are considered – that is, those with tumours not more than five centimetres in diameter with or without enlarged lymphatic glands in the armpit – 75 per cent are alive at 5 years. The type of operation seems to matter little: in one series the proportion of patients treated in Stage I alive after 5 years was 72 per cent after radical mastectomy and 71 per cent after simple mastectomy.

The traditional view that cancer of the breast is a more aggressive disease in the younger woman has been proved to be without foundation. The elderly often die from some unrelated disorder before metastases declare themselves; the young survive long enough for them to become apparent. It has been shown recently in following the fate of 3558 women with cancer of the breast over 19 years that of those who died aged 21–50 years the cause in 96 per cent was the malignant disease; while it was responsible for only 77 per cent of deaths in those over 50. Half of the eventual deaths from breast cancer in those aged 21–50 years took place within 11½ years, of those aged 51–70 years half had died within 7¼ years, and of those aged 71–100 in 4 years. Thus if all causes of death other than cancer of the breast are discounted, the aggressive qualities of the disease can be seen to increase with age.

Metastases occur after such a long latent period in women with cancer of the breast that the question has been asked whether it is ever curable. It has been reasonably argued that when the age-adjusted survival rate is constant then the expectation of life is the same as that of the normal population and this must indicate cure. It has been shown that the length of survival is closely related to the size of the tumour when treatment is started. If its diameter exceeds three centimetres but is less than six centimetres the 5-year survival is 60 per cent and at 10 years age-adjusted survival is 50 per cent and constant thereafter. For patients with tumours of three centimetres in diameter the 5-year survival is 65 per cent, the 10-year 55 per cent, and by 13 years the survival curve is constant at 50 per cent. It is reasonable to suppose that these patients can be considered cured after

Cancer of the breast

13 years. With tumours of two centimetres and one centimetre the 5-year survival figures are 75 per cent and 95 per cent, the 10-year 68 per cent and 92 per cent, and the 20-year figures 60 per cent and 80 per cent. Even after 20 years the curves have not flattened and thus it is argued that further deaths from the cancer may occur and it is not justifiable to speak of cure.

Whatever else these figures prove, they do show beyond all question that the smaller the tumour the greater the length of survival and thus the earlier diagnosis is made the better the outlook for the patient. To achieve this cancers must be identified before they cause symptoms and when only mammography will reveal them. This is yet another argument in favour of screening for cancer of the breast.

13

Cancer of the reproductive system

Cancer of the ovary

Cancer of the ovary caused the death of 3621 women in England and Wales in 1975, a number equivalent to 6.4 per cent of all dying of malignant disease in that year. For the same year, the mortality rate per 1 000 000 living was 143 and this figure has shown a progressive rise over the last half century; for the 5-year period 1911–15 it was only 28 per year. There has, therefore, been a five-fold increase in its frequency as a cause of death. The registration rate per year per 1 000 000 living was 141 for the period 1963–6, suggesting that this tumour is usually lethal. The increase in its frequency has not been limited to England and Wales, but has been noted in the United States and most countries in Western Europe. It remains, however, relatively rare in Japan and the Orient generally.

The majority of ovarian tumours are benign and various types of cyst are the most common. Several are liable to malignant change. Of cancers some 85 per cent are primary carcinomas and another 5 per cent are secondary to malignant disease elsewhere in the abdomen. The remaining 10 per cent include tumours which may exert endocrine activity, some have a 'masculinizing' effect by forming male sex hormones. The malignant ovarian tumours often affect both ovaries.

The cancer spreads locally becoming attached to and invading such neighbouring organs as the bladder and the bowel. These tumours have a particular tendency to shed cancer cells which become implanted on the peritoneal membrane covering the bowel and other organs within the abdominal cavity. These seedling growths cause exudation of fluid, the accumulation of which leads to distension of the abdomen. The lymphatic glands lying at the back of the abdominal cavity are often invaded early, but blood-borne metastases are rare and occur late in the course of the disease.

The ovaries lie deep within the lower part of the abdominal cavity and when affected by malignant disease symptoms often arise only when spread of the growth has taken place. There will be complaint of pains in the lower area of the abdomen, perhaps of disturbed bowel habit, and of uncomfortable distension. Examination at this stage will often reveal a swelling, although it may only be felt on internal examination. If fluid has accumulated within the abdomen it may be found to contain cancer cells if a specimen can be obtained by needle puncture. In general however the diagnosis can seldom be made with certainty without the surgeon exploring the swelling, removing it if possible and, if not, removing a fragment for microscopic examination.

The appropriate treatment depends upon the surgeon's finding at the time of operation. In 70 per cent of women with cancer of the ovary the growth is no longer localized, but has spread to other organs when the surgeon is first consulted. When possible the womb, the ovaries, and the Fallopian tubes are removed. When this is made impossible by local spread the choice lies between radiotherapy and chemotherapy, neither of which can be regarded as more than palliative. The sensitivity of these tumours is variable and the effects of radiotherapy uncertain. The results of chemotherapy are more encouraging. In some 50 per cent there is considerable improvement with shrinkage of the tumour when a single drug is used. Drug combinations have given remission rates of 80 per cent in previously untreated patients, but in no cases for longer than 18 months.

The outlook depends on the extent to which the growth has spread when treatment is undertaken. The proportion surviving after 5 years is 62 per cent if the cancer is limited to the ovary, 39 per cent if it has extended into the pelvis, 7 per cent if it has spread by seeding throughout the abdominal cavity, and nil when distant metastases are present.

The value of post-operative radiotherapy is debatable. In one series for the first three categories mentioned the survivals at 5 years were 62 per cent without post-operative irradiation and 58 per cent with, 19 per cent and 42 per cent and 11 per cent. These figures suggest that post-operative irradiation is worthwhile if the growth has spread outside the ovary.

Cancer of the womb

Malignant disease of the womb or uterus occurs at two sites, within the body of the organ and in its neck. The behaviour of these two tumours presents many points of difference and they require separate discussion.

Cancer of the body of the womb

This type of malignant disease arises from the cells of the glandular lining of the uterus. This tissue, called the endometrium, undergoes a regular succession of changes during the reproductive phase of woman's life, each cycle ending with a monthly period. Cancer of the body of the uterus is thus a carcinoma of the endometrium.

It is a disease predominantiy of the elderly. The median age at which it presents is 56 years and 75 per cent arise after the periods have ceased. It was the certified cause of death in 1165 women in England and Wales in 1975, accounting for 2.1 per cent of female deaths from cancer. The mortality rate in 1975 was 46 and it has shown little change over the period for which precise figures are available. The registered incidence per 1 000 000 per year was 133 for the period 1961–3, at which time the mortality rate was 50. This difference shows it to be a tumour which is frequently curable.

The cells of the endometrium from which this cancer arises are particularly sensitive to hormonal influences. It is, of course, the hormones formed by the ovaries that are responsible for the cyclical changes in them which underlie menstruation. Thus it is not surprising that endocrine factors should be important in the cause of cancer of the

Cancer of the organs of reproduction

endometrium. Women with this disease often have been found to conform to a characteristic pattern: they have usually passed the menopause; they are often overweight, commonly childless or even infertile, and suffer more than the average from diabetes and a raised blood pressure. It has been shown that prolonged dosage with a female sex hormone (oestrogen) will cause cancer of the endometrium in animals and the tumour will often respond to treatment with another and, in a sense antagonistic, hormone (progestogen). Excess oestrogen, whether of natural origin or given as a medication, causes an overgrowth of the cells of the endometrium which is recognized as a precancerous state. Indeed evidence has accrued recently to suggest that oestrogen given to control the symptoms of the change of life may be responsible for some cases of cancer of the body of the uterus.

Over 90 per cent of these cancers are carcinomas which arise from the cells of the endometrium as described in the preceding paragraphs. Other malignant tumours are quite exceptional. The carcinomas spread slowly, first invading the underlying muscular wall of the uterus and later the lymphatic glands in the pelvis and those on the back wall of the abdominal cavity. Blood-borne metastases are rare and late.

There is virtually only one symptom of cancer of the body of the womb and that is bleeding from the vagina after the periods have ended. In the 25 per cent of women in whom the disease arises before the change of life, there is bleeding at times other than at the period or continuous loss of blood. Internal examination may disclose enlargement of the womb, but even this sign of disease is often lacking.

Sometimes cancer cells can be identified in the bloody discharge from the womb, but the essential diagnostic step is dilatation and curettage, popularly abbreviated to 'D. & C'. Under an anaesthetic the gynaecologist stretches the narrow channel through the neck of the womb until he can pass a curette into the body of the organ. With this instrument he scrapes the endometrial lining to obtain tissue which is then examined microscopically. X-ray films taken after injection of radio-opaque material into the cavity of the womb have been advocated. They show the extent of the tumour, but have little practical value, for if a tumour is present whatever its size the womb must almost always be removed.

Two methods of curative treatment are available: surgery and radiotherapy. The second has been used in two forms: the introduction for a limited period of radium into the cavity of the uterus, and conventional deep X-ray therapy. Supervoltage therapy is rapidly displacing the first. The choice of treatment depends largely upon the extent of the tumour. When there is only precancerous change or where the growth is entirely confined to the cavity of the womb, simple removal of the uterus (hysterectomy) is sufficient; when the tumour has spread down to invade the neck of the womb, pre-operative radiotherapy is followed by hysterectomy; when there is spread into the pelvis, deep X-ray treatment followed by radical hysterectomy is usually advised. The outlook for these three grades in terms of the proportion surviving 5 years is as follows: 85–90 per cent, 50–65 per cent, and 30 per cent.

Once the growth has spread outside the pelvis, surgery has usually become impossible and reliance has to be placed on supervoltage radiotherapy. The proportion surviving after 5 years falls to less than 10 per cent. The overall 5-year survival of women with cancer of the endometrium is 53 per cent.

When metastases have formed, and the disease is disseminated, treatment with the female sex hormone progesterone will often control it for a considerable period. The action of this hormone can be regarded as antagonistic to that of oestrogen. In one series treatment with medroxyprogesterone led to complete disappearance of all symptoms and signs of disease in 11 per cent; a partial remission in 22 per cent; and relief of symptoms in 38 per cent.

Cancer of the organs of reproduction

Cancer of the neck of the womb

Cancer of the neck of the womb or the uterine cervix is one of the most important and common malignant diseases affecting women. It accounts for some 12 per cent of female cancers. It is often curable and it is the tumour most readily detected in its earlier stage by screening methods (see Chapter 7).

In 1975 it was the certified cause of death of 2143 women in England and Wales and accounted for 3.8 per cent of fatal cancers in this sex. The death rate, which has fallen recently, was 85. The first comparable figures are for the 5-year period 1951-5 when the death rate per year was 109. The difference between the registration and death rates bears witness to the curability of this cancer. For the period 1963-6 the registration rate was 179 per year per million living, and the death rate at this time 100.

Women with invasive cancer of the cervix average 45 years of age when they first present themselves for treatment, but there is a suggestion that the disease is now appearing at an earlier age.

There are a number of observations which have a bearing on the cause of this form of malignant disease. Considerable geographical variations in its frequency have been noted. It is more common when living standards are low and even in any one country it occurs more frequently in the lower socio-economic groups than in the higher. This may explain some of the geographical variation. For instance in the American negro it is 2.5 times more common than in the white American. However there are anomalies which it cannot explain. The last available figures showed the death rate per 1 000 000 living per year to be 100 in Sweden and 175 in Denmark. It is a rare disease in Israeli-born Jews and this has been attributed to Jewish males being circumcised.

There is general agreement that sexual activity predisposes to cancer of the cervix and the earlier intercourse begins and the more frequently it is undertaken the greater the risk. It is four times more common than the average in prostitutes.

It is rare in nuns: in a series of 13 000 Italian nuns who died there was no case of cancer of the cervix, but 14 of cancer of the body of the womb. In another analysis 45 per cent of women with cancer of the cervix were found to have married before the age of 20, while of those without this disease the proportion was only 24 per cent; 21 per cent with cancer of the cervix had been divorced and only 6 per cent of those not affected. There is a correlation between venereal diseases and this form of cancer. An odd observation showed it to be 2.5 times more common than the average in the wives of fishermen, deck hands, and engine-room ratings. Non-obstructive contraception appears to lessen the risk.

Interest has been aroused recently by a possible connection between a virus infection and cancer of the uterine cervix. It has been found that in 48–100 per cent of women with this tumour there is evidence of past infection with herpes simplex virus type II whereas this is so in only 18–67 per cent of normal women. This virus is thought to be transmitted venereally and thus its presence may be no more than evidence of early and frequent sexual intercourse.

Cancer of the cervix passes through three stages and some mention of these has been made in earlier chapters. The cervical smear test has shown that there is often an early precancerous stage described as 'dysplasia'; in this the cells of the membrane covering the cervix are abnormal and increase in number but are clearly not malignant. In about 1 case in 3 the process advances to the second stage which is known as 'carcinoma-in-situ'. Here the cells have acquired all the characteristics of malignancy but they have not invaded the underlying tissues and they appear incapable of spreading further or causing metastases (see Plate 16c). This may pass into the third stage of 'invasive carcinoma'. There is little doubt that a number of examples of carcinoma-in-situ resolve and do not advance to the invasive stage, but what proportion undergoes resolution is unknown. Cervical smear tests show that the average age at which dysplasia if found is 28 years; for carcinoma-in-situ it is 32 years; and for invasive carcinoma 45 years. These differences show the length of time frank cancer takes to develop.

In almost all cases the particular type of cancer is a carcinoma arising from the cells of the membrane covering the cervix. The growth may invade the cervix itself, it may appear as an ulcer, or it may project as a tumour into the vagina. It spreads locally invading the lymphatic glands in the neighbourhood and adjacent organs such as the bladder and rectum. Distant blood-borne metastases are rare.

Doctors recognize various stages of invasive cancer and this is helpful in deciding the appropriate treatment and in forecasting the outcome. In Stage I the growth is confined to the cervix; in Stage II it has spread beyond the cervix but has not reached the wall of the pelvis or the lower third of the vagina; in Stage III it has spread to these areas; and in Stage IV it has spread outside the pelvis and invaded the bladder or rectum.

Carcinoma of the cervix is now usually discovered early and before it affects health. There are no symptoms with dysplasia and none in 35–60 per cent of women with carcinoma-in-situ. Bleeding occurs in perhaps 20 per cent and is usually due to contact and thus commonly after sexual intercourse. Even in invasive carcinoma 30 per cent of women suffer no symptoms in Stage I. In 35–65 per cent contact bleeding is noted and later vaginal discharge often offensive and sometimes consisting of pus is the rule. Pain is a feature only of the later stages.

Nowadays the diagnosis is usually made in Stage I or earlier by means of the cervical smear. This procedure is discussed in Chapter 7. Examination in the later stages will reveal a tumour or ulcer of the cervix and will allow the extent of the growth to be assessed. Diagnosis is of course always established by microscopic examination of tissue removed from the growth or the suspicious area.

The treatment to be recommended varies with the stage of the cancer and often with the age of the patient. When the cervical smear test shows dysplasia some recommend removal of the womb if the dysplastic change is severe and if the woman has no wish for further children. Operation is sometimes limited to removal of a cone of tissue from the cervix which includes the dysplastic area. Some on the other hand recommend watching progress and repeating the smear test at intervals of 3 months. The same programme is suitable for those in whom the test shows carcinoma-in-situ although there is much to be said for operation in women over the age of 35 years without further reproductive ambitions.

With invasive carcinoma in Stage I removal of the uterus is the recognized treatment. In Stage II if the patient is young and fit a more radical operation removing the uterus, the upper part of the vagina, the ovaries and the tubes is often advised. The alternative and, in older or frail patients the preferable course, is to treat by radiotherapy. Radio-therapy which gives results comparable with those of surgery is to be advised in the more advanced stages. However, even when the whole pelvis is filled with tumour some surgeons carry out an operation of alarming magnitude which they describe as exenteration. It is said that as high a proportion as 20 per cent of those who survive are cured if all the tumour can be removed.

Cancer of the cervix uteri when diagnosed in an early stage is a curable disease. Using the stages described in an earlier paragraph the proportion of women living 5 years after the start of treatment are as follows: Stage I 70–85 per cent, Stage II 40–60 per cent, Stage III 30 per cent, and Stage IV 10 per cent. The overall survival after 5 years is 46 per cent.

Choriocarcinoma

The layer of cells forming the membrane which comes to enclose the developing foetus and which attaches it to the endometrium lining the cavity of the womb is called the trophoblast. It is from this that a rare type of cancer, the choriocarcinoma, arises. It is, of course, always associated with pregnancy although frequently with one which ends in abortion or is in some other way abnormal.

Cancer of the organs of reproduction

Choriocarcinoma occurs in about one pregnancy in 20000 in Europe and the United States, but in the Far East is much more common. In the Philippines it is reported once in every 1380 pregnancies. It was the certified cause of death in only 7 women in England and Wales in 1975, but this figure does not represent its true frequency for many are now cured. It is a highly malignant form of cancer seldom seen after the age of 35 years. It rapidly invades the muscular layer of the womb and gives rise early to distant metastases. The usual initial symptom is irregular bleeding from the vagina. Diagnosis is established by microscopic examination of curettings.

Although of great rarity choriocarcinoma is of interest to those who study malignant disease for two reasons. First, it is one of the few tumours which can be cured by chemotherapy. It is particularly sensitive to a drug called methotrexate and even when the disease is generalized 75 per cent of patients can be cured. Secondly, the malignant trophoblastic cells form a hormone known as chorionic gonadotrophin. The quantity of this substance in the blood can be accurately measured and this provides an index of whether all the cancer cells have been destroyed or not.

Cancer of the vagina

Cancer of the vagina is a rare disease from which only 128 women in England and Wales died in 1975. The mortality rate for that year was 5 per 1 000 000 living. It rarely occurs below the age of 50 years and, with the exception mentioned later, almost always arises from the lining epithelium of the vagina: it is, in pathological terms, a squamous-cell carcinoma.

The common site of origin is in the upper and hinder part of the vagina where it forms an ulcer which causes bleeding and discharge; often there are two or more growths. Biopsy establishes the diagnosis. Local spread is through the vaginal wall into the pelvis and to the lymphatic glands of the region.

Treatment, when the disease is completely localized, may be surgical or by irradiation often by application of radium. When there is extensive spread into the pelvic tissues only

radiotherapy is practicable. In the localized type the proportion surviving after 5 years is 70 per cent, but where there
is extension into the pelvis it drops to 27 per cent.

The exception to which reference is made earlier is a cancer
arising from glandular cells which has been noted in teenaged
girls whose mothers have been treated with a hormone-like
drug, diethylstilboestrol, in pregnancy. In the past this
preparation has been extensively prescribed in the hopes of
controlling the habitual tendency to miscarriage which
affects some women. The association, which has only been
appreciated within the past 5 years, has been discussed in an
earlier chapter (Chapter 2).

Cancer of the vulva

Cancer of the vulva is a disease of the elderly and is seen most
often in the seventh decade. It was the certified cause of
death in 408 women in England and Wales in 1975 when
the mortality rate was 16 per million living.

In pathological terms the tumour is almost always a
squamous-cell carcinoma arising from the covering epithelium.
In between 20 and 45 per cent malignant changes develop
simultaneously in several areas. Its appearance is often preceded by precancerous changes of which there are several
varieties. The most common are leukoplakia, similar to the
precancerous change described in the mouth (Chapter 9),
kraurosis, a condition in which the epithelium becomes
thinned and dry, and the chronic inflammation often seen in
diabetics. The cancer spreads locally and, if neglected, may
extend as far as the anus. Lymphatic glands in the groin are
often invaded early.

The early symptoms are irritation, pain, and bleeding. It
is characteristic of this disease that patients seek medical
advice late, regarding the symptoms as one of the inevitable
disabilities of old age. Diagnosis is seldom difficult and can
readily be confirmed by biopsy.

The appropriate treatment depends upon the extent of
the growth. When localized and superficial irradiation or

surgery is curative; when some invasion has taken place, more radical operation is required; when curative surgery is clearly impossible or when the patient's health precludes operation radiotherapy is indicated.

Many sufferers from cancer of the vulva are old and frail, the disease is often extensive when help is sought and the survivors after 5 years are few. In women under the age of 50 the overall survival rate 5 years after treatment is 60 per cent.

Cancer of the testicle

Cancer of the testicle was certified as the cause of death of 241 men in England and Wales in 1975, giving a mortality rate for the year of 10 per 1 000 000. The curability of this tumour is shown by the registration rate of 22 per 1 000 000 per year for the period 1963-6. There has been a moderate increase in the numbers dying from this disease over the years: the mortality rate per year for the period 1911-15 was 5 per 1 000 000 living. The incidence does not differ widely throughout the world. It arises most often between the ages of 20 and 40 years. In the process of development the testicle descends from a position just below the kidney to lie at birth in the scrotum. Its descent may be held up at any point and the risk of cancer arising in a misplaced testicle is said to be 200 times greater than in one normally situated.

From the pathological standpoint there are two groups of testicular cancer, each of which has been divided into several subtypes. The first category is that of the seminomas where the growth arises from the cells which form the sperms, and the second that of the teratomas. A teratoma is a tumour which originates from cells which normally disappear during the development of the foetus, but which sometimes persist into adult life. Eighty per cent of testicular tumours are seminomas and 20 per cent teratomas.

The cancer spreads by the lymphatic vessels accompanying the spermatic cord, which leaves the upper end of the testicle to enter the abdomen carrying the duct for the sperm as well as arteries and veins. Through this pathway malignant cells reach the lymphatic glands on the back wall of the abdominal cavity early and spread upwards. Metastases in the lungs are common; they are found less frequently in the liver.

Almost always the patient consults his doctor because he has felt a swelling in one testicle. Confirmation usually requires surgical exploration, lymphangiographic studies (see Chapter 6) will determine the presence or absence of enlarged lymphatic glands within the abdomen, and an X-ray film of the chest excludes metastases in the lungs.

The seminoma is a less malignant tumour than the teratoma and in some centres the two are treated differently. In the case of a seminoma the testicle is removed and the lymphatic glands lying along the back wall of the abdomen treated by radiotherapy whether there is evidence that they are invaded by cancer or not. It is known that even when no sign of spread to these glands exists they contain cancer cells in 10 per cent of seminomas and 25–30 per cent of teratomas. Some treat teratoma by removal of the testicle and by excising the potentially affected lymphatic glands even when there is no evidence that they are diseased. This is carried out as a preventive measure. If they are obviously infiltrated by cancer, radiotherapy perhaps with chemotherapy is prescribed. Many recommend removal of misplaced testicles because of the risk of their becoming cancerous, especially if they are shrunken and non-functioning.

The seminoma is strikingly sensitive to chemotherapy and radiotherapy and when localized to the testicle the survival after 5 years is 85–90 per cent. When the lymphatic glands are affected the figure falls to 20–30 per cent and when there are metastases to 5–15 per cent. The group of teratomas carries a less favourable outlook and it is in this area that chemotherapy is proving valuable. Various drugs and drug combinations have been advocated. In one series 30 per cent of a series of men with advanced generalized teratoma were alive and free from disease 2 years after treatment. The overall survival rate at 5 years in men with teratoma is is 48 per cent; when the cancer is limited to the testicle and there is no spread to the glands the figure is 55–65 per cent.

Cancer of the penis

Cancer of the penis is a rare disease in England and Wales where it was the certified cause of death of 102 men in 1975 with a mortality rate of 2 per 1 000 000 living. It has become rather less common over the past 50 years, but there is great geographical variation. It is frequent in Asia, particularly in Chinese and Javanese and, in the natives of Uganda, it is said to be the cancer most often encountered.

Cancer of the penis is virtually unknown in those who have been circumcised in infancy and in general it appears to be related to lack of personal hygiene. Pathologically it is a squamous-cell carcinoma and arises either at the end of the organ or on the foreskin. It invades the underlying tissue and spreads by lymphatic channels first to the glands in the groin and thence to those within the abdomen.

Diagnosis requires little more than inspection, but must be confirmed by biopsy. The treatment required depends upon its extent. If entirely localized and superficial and unaccompanied by enlarged lymphatic glands, simple excision or radiotherapy is curative and 90 per cent will be alive after 5 years. If there is deeper local infiltration more extensive surgery is required and the survival rate falls to 50–70 per cent. When the lymphatic glands in the groin are enlarged, surgical treatment of the primary tumour is followed by their excision and post-operative radiotherapy: the survival rate at 5 years is about 35 per cent. Overall the proportion of survivors after 5 years is 32 per cent.

14

Leukaemia and lymphoma

Leukaemia and lymphoma make up a group of interrelated malignant diseases which present notable differences from other forms of cancer. They arise from cells of what are called the lympho-reticular tissues. These cells are not gathered into neat anatomical packets to form circumscribed organs, but are scattered throughout the body. In the tumours which arise from them the cells have characteristics recognized as cancerous, but some hallmarks of malignancy, such as infiltration and metastasis, may be lacking. For many years the very nature of these disorders was subject to debate, but their unrestrained growth and aggressive behaviour have convinced all that they are to be regarded as truly cancerous.

All the cells of the lympho-reticular tissue are believed to spring from one primordial ancestor, but during the course of development they undergo changes which fit them for their several, and often limited, specific functions. Except for the production of the red blood cells, these are mainly concerned with the protection of the body against harmful intruders. They fall into two main categories: those from which the red blood cells and the granular and monocytic families of white blood cell are formed, and those which give rise to the other strain of leukocyte or white blood cell, the lymphocyte. Representatives of all these circulate in the blood, but after birth those of the first group are otherwise confined in health to the bone marrow, while the lymphocytes make up the lymphatic glands and the spleen as well as being found in small collections in many other tissues. Each group is best regarded as a 'system' composed of some cells fixed in position, but constantly dividing to form others which mature and are set free in the blood. In health the number of each type of blood cell in a cubic millimetre of blood is kept within a constant narrow range. For red blood cells this averages 5 000 000. The myeloid or granular white blood cells, so called because they contain minute granules, total some 4000 per cubic millimetre. The average life of a red blood cell is about 120 days and of a granular white blood cell 15 hours: as they perish they are replaced by new cells formed in the bone marrow. The monocytic family of leukocytes – the monocytes – number only 500 per cubic millimetre. They leave the circulation within 36 hours and lodge in tissues throughout the body where they play the part of scavengers removing debris from areas of inflammation or degeneration. In their new positions they are known as histiocytes or macrophages. Lymphocytes are in constant circulation from their sites of origin, through the lymphatic channels into the blood and back to the tissues from which they arose. They number about 2500 per cubic millimetre and their survival is variable. Some are short-lived, perishing within 3 or 4 days, others live for many years.

Leukaemia

Leukaemia is sometimes described as 'cancer of the blood', a term which contributes only further confusion to a subject already sufficiently complex. The fundamental change is a malignant alteration, a cancer, in the 'fixed' cells from which the leukocytes are formed. Massive proliferation of these cells usually leads to a greatly enhanced production of their apparently normal mature descendants which in many instances enter the blood in vastly increased numbers accompanied by immature precursors that normally remain 'fixed'. It was this flooding of the circulating blood with mature and immature white blood cells which led the German pathologist, Virchow, to give the disease the name of *'weisses Blut'* or leukaemia, but the phenomenon must be regarded as a common side-effect of the underlying disorder and not as a constant or necessary feature.

There are several varieties of leukaemia and they are classified in two ways. First, by the course of the disease into acute and chronic, and secondly by the strain of leukocyte affected. Acute and chronic myeloid or granulocytic leukaemias and acute and chronic lymphatic leukaemias make up the great majority, although there are a number of less common variants. The several types have many points of difference, but there are certain general aspects of leukaemia which require discussion first.

It is difficult to speak with confidence of the incidence of leukaemia except in countries where the standards of medicine are sufficiently high to provide the sophisticated methods and technical expertise required for its diagnosis. Incidence can be deduced from the mortality rates, because unhappily leukaemia is still usually a fatal disease. In 1975, 3194 deaths were certified as due to leukaemia in England and Wales, giving a mortality rate of 65 per 1 000 000 living. 1753 of these deaths were of men and 1441 of women giving mortality rates for the two sexes of 73 and 57 per 1 000 000 living. There is little difference between the rates in this country, those of other Western European nations and of the United States. The disease appears more common in the north of Europe, than in the south, although in the British Isles it is seen less often in Scotland than in the southern counties of England. There are ethnic variations within countries: for example it is 2.4 times more common in Jewish American children than in non-Jewish.

The frequency of the several varieties differs in the East and West. In England and Wales in 1975, 58 per cent of the deaths from this disease were certified as due to acute leukaemia, 24 per cent to chronic lymphatic leukaemia, and 18 per cent to chronic granulocytic leukaemia. In Japan the proportion of chronic lymphatic leukaemia is only 2.5 per cent. The different types vary too in the age at which they make their appearance and their incidence upon the two sexes. In children almost all leukaemia is of the acute variety: below the age of 15 years it ranks as the fourth most common cause of death with an age-adjusted mortality rate of 25 per 1 000 000 living. It is exceeded only by accidents, congenital heart disease, and acute chest infections. Almost always it is of the lymphatic variety: 49 per cent of those dying from this disease are aged less than 15 years and 65 per cent are boys. Other types of acute leukaemia are spread evenly throughout the span of life. Chronic granulocytic leukaemia is a disease of the middle years, appearing most often about the age of 45 and 54 per cent being in males. The incidence of chronic lymphatic leukaemia reaches a peak 10 years later and 59 per cent of its victims are male.

There is a widespread belief that leukaemia is more common than formerly. In the United States the numbers certified as dying of this disease increased four-fold between 1921 and 1951. Similar increases were recorded in all Western countries. Since then there has been a small reduction. In England and Wales the standardized mortality ratio, taken as 100 in 1968, had fallen by 1973 to 98 for males and 89 for females. The apparent increase has been chiefly in the elderly and, although more precise diagnoses and improved care of old persons play a part, it seems likely that in this group it is real.

A number of factors have been suspected of initiating the malignant process that results in leukaemia. On an analogy with 'carcinogenic' these can reasonably be termed 'leukaemogenic'. It has long been thought that genetic influences were of importance. Acute leukaemia and chronic lymphatic leukaemia certainly occur more frequently in members of the same family than would be expected. It has been claimed that when one of a pair of identical twins develops acute leukaemia, the second is eventually affected in 25 per cent of cases.

The chromosomes, the minute rod-like bodies in the nuclei of cells, which carry the genes, may present abnormalities in acute leukaemia. This disease occurs more frequently than expected in a variety of disorders marked by chromosomal abnormality. Mongolism, for example, known to be constantly associated with a characteristic aberration of one particular chromosome, carries a risk of acute leukaemia fifteen times that of normal. In chronic granulocytic leukaemia there is in

159

almost every case a specific chromosomal abnormality in the leukaemic white blood cells. Although some association is evident, the nature of the link between leukaemia and these chromosomal abnormalities is unknown.

In some animals – the fowl, the mouse, and the cat – leukaemia is undoubtedly of viral origin. In man the evidence of a viral cause, in spite of diligent research, is no more than suggestive.

The most clearly attested leukaemogen is undoubtedly ionizing radiation. It was discussed briefly in Chapter 2. Nearly 50 years ago it was found that exposure of mice to X-rays increased the incidence of leukaemia twelve-fold. Even before that time frequent reports had been published of the disease in those who pioneered the diagnostic use of X-rays. The validity of this view has been established most convincingly by the consequences of the atomic bomb attacks in Japan in 1945. In survivors who were less than 1000 metres from the centre of the explosion leukaemia was sixty times more frequent than expected. The peak of incidence was recorded between 1950 and 1955 and by 1965 the level in Hiroshima had returned to that of the rest of Japan. Other evidence is to be found in a study of men treated for a form of arthritis of the spine by radiotherapy: follow-up showed that in them the incidence of leukaemia was 9.5 times that expected and that it commonly arose between 5 and 10 years after treatment.

The relationship between ionizing radiation and leukaemia appears a simple 'linear' one. There is no dose so small that it has no influence and the risk increases *pari passu* with the dose of radiation received. Nevertheless the importance of preserving a sense of proportion should be stressed: the risk of leukaemia after radiation is still less than that of crossing a busy street.

Finally, there are some drugs and other chemical agents the use of which has been followed by leukaemia. The most clear-cut example is benzene, but many others have been accused usually on insufficient evidence. More important is the observation that prolonged chemotherapy for some other types of cancer may be followed by the development of leukaemia.

In almost all the instances cited above the leukaemia is of the acute, or less often chronic, granulocytic type. It does appear that lymphatic leukaemia cannot be accounted for by recognizable leukaemogens. It is true too that in not more than 5 per cent of leukaemic patients can a history of exposure to any known leukaemogenic agent be elicited.

Acute leukaemia

The several varieties of acute leukaemia are best considered together, because the pattern of illness caused by the different types shows few differences and their distinction rests largely with the laboratory.

This malignant disease affects the earliest ancestors of the two kinds of white blood cell. It will be readily appreciated that since they are at one stage all products of the same ancestor difficulties often arise in deciding whether a primitive cell should be regarded as belonging to the granulocytic or to the lymphocytic series. It is only when development has reached a certain stage that distinction between the two can confidently be made. The most primitive identifiable cell of the granular or myeloid series is known as the myeloblast and that of the lymphocytic strain as the lymphoblast; the two common forms of acute leukaemia are therefore sometimes described as myeloblastic and lymphoblastic. Characteristically in acute leukaemia the bone-marrow is crowded with primitive cells of one or other of these varieties and variable numbers of them overflow into the blood. Sometimes the total number of white blood cells circulating in the blood is greatly reduced perhaps to less than 2000 per cubic millimetre; sometimes it is immensely increased to 200 000 or more per cubic millimetre. In either case myeloblasts or lymphoblasts can be identified and may make up 99 per cent of all the cells when the total number is greatly raised, or when reduced only 5–10 per cent.

161

Acute granulocytic leukaemia is the commoner of the two. In England and Wales in 1975, 607 men and 556 women making a total of 1163 persons were certified as dying from this disease, giving a mortality rate of 23 per 1 000 000 living. 380 persons were certified as dying of acute lymphocytic leukaemia in this year and of these 60 per cent were male. The overall mortality rate for the year was 8 per 1 000 000 living. The striking contrast lies in the different ages at which the two diseases appear: 3.4 per cent of males and 4.6 per cent of females dying of acute granulocytic leukaemia were below the age of 15 years, but in the acute lymphoblastic form the proportions were 52 per cent and 44 per cent. Indeed, 49 per cent of all deaths from the second were in persons below 15 years of age. The age adjusted mortality rates per 1 000 000 for this age group were males 20 and females 12 for acute lymphocytic leukaemia and 3 and 5 for the acute granulocytic type.

The illness caused by the two types and at different ages is similar. It may start insidiously with lassitude, shortness of breath, and general malaise. Sometimes a sore throat or feverish illness from which the anticipated recovery seems unduly delayed is the opening event. Sometimes a nose bleed or an unexplained liability to bruise first arouses suspicion. Examination will disclose pallor, perhaps abnormal bruising, and possible minor enlargement of the spleen and lymphatic glands. Diagnosis depends on examination of the blood and bone-marrow. The first will show anaemia and the presence of the lymphoblasts or myeloblasts mentioned earlier; the bone marrow will have been overrun by these cells. The distinction between acute lymphoblastic and acute myeloblastic leukaemia, once only of academic concern, has become important because the two diseases require different types of treatment and carry a different outlook. In many there is little or no difficulty, but there is a significant proportion in which the differentiation demands great experience and technical expertise.

The last 20 years have seen revolutionary developments in

the treatment of acute leukaemia. These have an interest far beyond their application to this particular disease because it is from the lessons learned in the treatment of leukaemias and lymphomas that many of the advances in the chemotherapy of cancer have sprung.

The treatment of acute leukaemia is prolonged and arduous, making demands upon the patient and his relatives which must at times seem intolerable. There is no question that experience and expertise are of such importance that it is no longer justifiable to treat the patient with acute leukaemia anywhere but in a specialized centre. It is impossible, even if it were desirable, to conceal the diagnosis from the adult patient and seldom indeed from a child, for treatment cannot be undertaken without his informed appreciation and co-operation.

The first phase of treatment aims to restore the blood, bone-marrow, and physical health to normal. When this has been achieved it is spoken of as 'remission' but a large mass of leukaemic cells is known to remain. The second phase attempts to destroy this malignant residue and the third, although often called that of maintenance, continues the systematic eradication of leukaemic tissue. Although the principles for treating the two forms of acute leukaemia are similar the details differ considerably.

In acute lymphocytic leukaemia remission is induced by treatment with a cortisone-like drug, prednisolone, and another agent called vincristine. In 80–95 per cent all signs of disease and all abnormalities in the blood have disappeared after 3 or 4 weeks. The course of treatment is repeated twice in the hopes of eradicating as much leukaemic tissue as possible. This is followed by radiotherapy in the shape of irradiation of the skull and the spinal cord. Residual leukaemic cells are often to be found in the nervous system where they seem to be out of reach of antileukaemic drugs; if irradiation is omitted a high proportion relapse with signs of damage to the brain or spinal cord. When radiotherapy is concluded intermittent courses of antileukaemic drugs are continued for 130 weeks. If there are still no signs of recurrence treatment is then discontinued.

Cancer – the facts

In one series of children 50 per cent were well and free from signs of disease 5 years after starting treatment. The results in adults are less good than in children. It is difficult to know when one can safely speak of 'cure', but most would agree that when all is well after 7 years from the start of treatment it is pardonable to claim 'probable cure'. Twenty-five years ago the average length of survival in acute leukaemia was 3 months.

In acute granulocytic leukaemia the outlook is less good. The initial treatment consists of courses lasting 5 days during which a combination of drugs is given; they are separated by intervals of 7–10 days. The drugs used usually include dauno-rubicin and cytarabin; some centres add further agents. These powerful compounds destroy the leukaemic cells, but cause considerable damage also to the normal blood-forming tissue. Usually three courses of treatment are required before all signs of leukaemia disappear, but this complete remission is only achieved in 50–60 per cent of patients. It is followed by a critical period before the normal blood-forming cells have recovered. During this time anaemia progresses, the body's defences against infection are greatly impaired, and there is often a liability to bleed. Once this phase has been overcome and the blood has returned to normal, irradiation of the skull and spinal cord follow and then maintenance treatment with various drug combinations is undertaken. Unhappily relapse is only too frequent and the average survival of those achieving complete remission is about 50 weeks. Nevertheless recovery – although rare – does sometimes occur and every large centre can claim a few patients who appear to have been cured of acute granulocytic leukaemia.

The methods which have just been outlined are what may optimistically be called the 'curative' treatment. In addition supportive treatment is required and is of particular import-ance in the critical stage described as following induced remission in acute granulocytic leukaemia. Blood transfusion to repair anaemia will almost certainly be needed at some time in the course of the disease. The main risk is that of infection. Antileukaemic treatment causes such profound, although temporary, impairment of the body's defences that resistance to invasion by microbes virtually disappears and energetic treatment with antibiotics is often required.

Chronic granulocytic leukaemia

In chronic granulocytic leukaemia the cancerous proliferation of the granular strain of white blood cells occurs at a more mature level than in the acute form. In consequence the blood and bone-marrow are flooded with representatives of all the developmental stages of the series from small numbers of the most immature to many thousands of fully ripe cells.

Chronic granulocytic leukaemia accounts for about one-fifth of all leukaemias. In 1975, 291 men and 251 women in England and Wales were certified as dying from this disease and the mortality rates per 1 000 000 living for the year were 12 and 10. There has been no change in these rates since 1967 when comparable figures first became available. It is generally held to be most common between the ages of 30 and 60 years. It is rare in children, about 2.5 occurring before the age of 10 years. Age adjusted mortality rates show that its frequency as a cause of death increases with age in men: in those aged 45–54 the rate was 14 per 1 000 000 living and in those aged 75–84, 87. In the later ages it is twice as common in men as in women. This form of leukaemia has no racial predelictions and the only recognized causal factor is ionizing radiation.

The onset of the disease is often stealthy with lassitude, loss of weight, and shortness of breath. There may be dragging pain under the ribs on the left side resulting from enlargement of the spleen which may also cause a sense of distension. Examination reveals great enlargement of the spleen, in health, this organ, which lies beneath the lower ribs on the left, cannot be felt; in this disease it often reaches down to the level of the navel. Sometimes the patient consults his doctor because he has himself felt the massive enlargement of the organ or noticed a swelling while lying in his bath.

165

Examination of the blood establishes the diagnosis. The numbers of red blood cells are often moderately reduced, but the most striking change is an immense increase in the number of leukocytes. In 80 per cent of patients when first examined the leukocytes exceed 100 000 per cubic millimetre. Ninety-five per cent or more of these cells belong to the granular series: perhaps 40 per cent will be mature forms of a kind normally found in the circulating blood, immature cells ordinarily confined to the bone-marrow make up the rest in proportions gradually diminishing as they become less mature. Special methods will reveal the abnormal chromosome mentioned earlier in this chapter.

Many forms of treatment have been employed in chronic granulocytic leukaemia and most of them will lead to remission with disappearance of all symptoms, shrinkage of the spleen so that it can no longer be felt, and a return of the blood to normal. These remissions, however, never amount to cure, for after a variable period there is relapse and eventually the time comes when the disease no longer responds to treatment. At this stage the tempo of the malignant process increases. The blood comes to resemble that of acute granulocytic leukaemia with an overwhelming proportion of the most primitive cells, the spleen increases in size, the patient grows increasingly ill, thin, and weak, and the final curtain falls a few weeks or, at most, months after the onset of this acute phase.

At present therefore this disease must be regarded as incurable. Nevertheless it is usually possible to maintain remission until the illness enters the final phase. In remission the patient feels well and is able to lead a full and active life.

For some 50 years up to 1955 the accepted treatment was radiotherapy. Irradiation of the spleen would cause it to shrink and lead to complete remission. After a while relapse would take place and further remission could be induced by more radiotherapy. This sequence would be repeated perhaps two or three times before signs of the acute malignant phase made their appearance. In 1955 a new drug, busulphan, was introduced which was quite as effective in inducing remission as radiotherapy and could also be used for its maintenance until overwhelmed by the final malignant phase. It is now the standard treatment, but requires expert management for overdosage may cause damage to the blood-forming cells and progressive anaemia which may prove fatal. Rarely treatment with busulphan leads to a darkening of the skin and occasionally to serious lung complications. These sequels are so rare that in an inevitably fatal disease they do not justify denying patients the undoubted benefit treatment with busulphan carries.

Once the final phase of accelerated malignancy has been reached there is little that can be done to stem its advance. It is usually treated along the same lines as acute granulocytic leukaemia, but even transient remissions are few.

Removal of the spleen early in the course of the disease has been recommended by some. A controlled trial is in progress at present in the hopes of determining the value of this measure. It is hoped that operation will at least remove a considerable mass of cancerous tissue and avoid the discomfort of a vastly enlarged spleen in the later stages of the disease.

The survival of sufferers from chronic granulocytic leukaemia has shown little increase in the last 25 years. It was estimated then that 50 per cent lived 2.7 years. Several recent reports put the figure as between 1 and 3.8 years. In a carefully observed series of patients recently the average survival of those receiving radiotherapy was 2 years and 3 months and of those treated with busulphan 3 years and 3 months. The proportion alive after 5 years is recorded by different authors as between 5 and 17 per cent. It seems likely that the length of survival is slowly increasing. Women live on an average a year longer than men.

Chronic lymphocytic leukaemia

In chronic lymphocytic leukaemia there is a malignant proliferation of lymphocytes in the lymphatic glands, the spleen, the bone-marrow, and in other tissues where collections of these cells normally exist. Associated with this proliferation the number of lymphocytes in the blood increases. The separation of this disorder from some of those discussed later under the head of lymphoma is somewhat artificial. Microscopic examination of a lymphatic gland from a patient with chronic lymphatic leukaemia may show appearances identical with those of a gland from some types of lymphoma. The only distinction is that in the first there has been an escape of an excessive number of lymphocytes into the blood. Nevertheless there are points of difference between typical examples of the two disorders.

In 1975 chronic lymphatic leukaemia was the certified cause of death of 425 men and 295 women in England and Wales, giving mortality rates for the year of 18 and 12 per 1 000 000 living. Comparable figures are only available since 1967 when the rates were 14 and 9. This suggests a possible slight increase. It accounts for 24 per cent of deaths due to leukaemia. The average age at which patients first consult their doctors with this disease is 55 years, but the mortality rates show a striking increase with advancing years. The age adjusted rate in men aged 45–54 was 7 and in those aged 75–84, 176. In the earlier years the proportion of men to women is 1.4 to 1, but later this increases to 2 to 1. It is rare below the age of 40 years and virtually never occurs in children.

The cause of chronic lymphocytic leukaemia is unknown. Some have doubted whether it should be regarded as a cancerous process, but general opinion is firmly in favour of this view. A history of this disease in more than one member of the family, although rare, is commoner than with other types of leukaemia. In one series it amounted to 7 per cent. It is common in Europe and the United States and is said to be more frequent in those of Jewish blood. It is rare in the Far East probably for racial rather than geographical reasons. Of indigenes dying of leukaemia in Japan only 2.9 per cent had chronic lymphatic leukaemia, but in Americans of European stock the proportion was 31.5 per cent.

Leukaemia and lymphoma

The symptoms of this disease are insidious in onset with vague ill-health, disinclination for effort, and loss of weight. Indeed in 15–20 per cent the diagnosis is first revealed by a blood test carried out for some unrelated reason. Sometimes advice is sought because the patient has noted some enlarged lymphatic glands, or a skin rash has made its appearance.

Examination discloses enlarged lymphatic glands in some 80 per cent of patients when they are first seen. There is enlargement of the spleen, usually of moderate degree, in 75 per cent and enlargement of the liver in 50 per cent. The diagnosis is established by examination of the blood. In about half the red blood cells are reduced in number, but seldom more than a little. The white blood cells are increased due to an excess of lymphocytes, the number of which must exceed 5000 per cubic millimetre to satisfy the accepted definition of chronic lymphatic leukaemia. In most instances the figure is above 10 000 per cubic millimetre. Examination of the bone-marrow shows a similar excess of lymphocytes.

The course of this disease is often protracted. Health may be unimpaired for years, but slow deterioration eventually begins. The lymphatic glands grow in size, the red blood cells decrease in number until there is significant anaemia, the number of lymphocytes in the blood steadily rises often coming to exceed 100 000 per cubic millimetre, and resistance to infections increases. The end comes often after 6 or more years from anaemia, infection, or exhaustion.

There is no convincing evidence that treatment prolongs the life of those with chronic lymphocytic leukaemia. Nevertheless it undoubtedly makes life more tolerable and this, in a disease which lasts for many years, is an important consideration. In the early stages when there are few or no symptoms specific treatment is often best witheld. However even the most philosophical will often find it hard to accept with equanimity the opinion that he has leukaemia, which he knows to be a fatal disease, but that no treatment is contemplated. Nevertheless if it be accepted that treatment does no more than relieve symptoms, it is logical that none be prescribed if no symptoms exist.

169

The main indications for active treatment are advancing anaemia, enlargement of lymphatic glands causing aesthetic or mechanical embarrassment, and such complications as infection. There are several effective weapons. The cortisone-like drugs will often reduce the size of the glands and spleen and improve the anaemia, but they undoubtedly increase the risk of infection. Chemotherapy, using one of the nitrogen-mustard group of drugs such as chlorambucil or cyclophos-phamide, will often cause the glands and spleen to shrink, but may aggravate the anaemia. Radiotherapy has been in use for many years as a means of reducing the size of lymphatic glands. It will also reduce the numbers of lymphocytes if the spleen is irradiated, but there is some reason to suppose that it may actually shorten survival.

Considerable experience is needed to obtain the most favourable results from the available agents while avoiding the undesirable effects their use may occasion. In most centres reliance is placed on the judicious use of chemo-therapy and the cortisone-like drugs.

Supportive treatment is of major importance. It includes the use of blood transfusion when there is anaemia which cannot be otherwise repaired and the prompt use of the appropriate antibiotic when infection occurs. Removal of the spleen is undoubtedly beneficial in some patients when there is intractable anaemia or severe pain from its massive enlargement.

Half of all patients with chronic lymphocytic leukaemia live for 6 years, but many survive much longer. Twenty years is not unduly rare and 35 years has been recorded. It is a disease of later life and it is not surprising that 1 patient in 3 dies of some disease unrelated to his leukaemia. Of those who die from, rather than with, this disease, one-half are alive after 9 years. About one-half eventually succumb to infection. Younger patients live longer than older and women than men.

Malignant disorders of the cells forming red blood cells

The cells responsible for the formation of the red blood cells, like those from which the leukocytes spring, are liable to comparable malignant proliferations. They are considerably rarer than leukaemia, although acute and chronic forms are recognized.

The acute type is known as acute erythraemia, or after the Italian physician who first described it, as di Guglielmo's disease. It causes an illness indistinguishable from acute leukaemia except that the blood contains numerous immature and abnormal red blood cells. It is treated in the same way as acute granulocytic leukaemia to which it is closely related. The outlook is of the same order or even less favourable.

The chronic variant is more common. It is known by the cumbersome title of polycythaemia rubra vera or, after those who first described it, as Vaquez–Osler's disease. It usually makes its appearance between the ages of 40 and 60 years. The incidence is said to lie between 6 and 16 per 1 000 000 living but in 1975 it was the certified cause of death of only 66 men and 56 women in England and Wales and the mortality rates per 1 000 000 living were 2.7 for men and 2.2 for women. It is said to be more common in those of Jewish race.

It usually starts insidiously with headache, giddiness, loss of concentration, and symptoms often erroneously considered neurotic. A high colour or bloodshot eyes may give rise to comment and those with this disease have a complexion which is brick-red in summer and plum-coloured in winter. On examination, apart from the high colour, the only abnormality is an enlarged spleen. The blood test shows a great increase in the number of red blood cells, often to as many as 10 000 000 per cubic millimetre.

The disease often runs a protracted course, but the viscid blood greatly increases the risk of clotting in the arteries and veins. Thus stroke (cerebral thrombosis), heart attack (coronary thrombosis), and gangrene of a toe or a limb are possible complications which may lead to an unexpectedly early conclusion.

There is at present no cure and the aim of treatment is to reduce the number of red blood cells being made sufficiently to restore their numbers to normal and to maintain them at that level. Perhaps the most generally accepted method is by treatment with radioactive phosphorus which is deposited in the bone marrow irradiating it from within and restraining its excessive activity. It seems likely that this treatment increases the danger of the disease finishing as leukaemia: the risk is hard to assess because this conclusion is seen even without radiotherapy. There are drugs, of which busulphan (see p.166) is the most convenient and effective.

Although survivals for 20 years are reported, without treatment one-half of patients are dead in 18 months, of which about half die as a result of the clotting tendency. With radiotherapy half survive for 12 years and in those treated with radioactive phosphorus survival averages 4 years more than in those receiving any other form of treatment. An American physician has commented that 'most people would prefer some risk of dying of leukaemia at an advanced age, to that of dying younger without leukaemia'.

Myelomatosis

Myelomatosis, or multiple myeloma, is a malignant disease of plasma cells. The plasma cell is a descendant of the lymphocyte and when malignant changes develop the disorder is usually limited to the bone-marrow where innumerable tumours of cancerous plasma cells arise, often weakening or destroying bones.

It is a disease of the elderly, the peak of incidence being at 65 years. It appears to be growing more common. In England and Wales in 1945, 71 persons were certified as dying of myelomatosis, in 1975 the figure was 1308. The deaths per 1 000 000 living were 19 in 1956 and in 1975, 27. The sexes are equally affected. It is a disease which demands technical expertise for its diagnosis and it is the development of these methods which almost certainly accounts for much of the apparent increase in its frequency.

Nothing is known of its causation, but there may be some racial factors which predispose to it for it is twice as common in the American negro as in his white fellow countryman.

It causes variable patterns of illness. Perhaps most often the first symptoms are those which result from anaemia due to the bone-marrow tumours destroying the blood-forming cells. Easy bruising often accompanies this. At other times pain in the bones or even spontaneous fractures are features. The disease can lead to disorder of the kidneys and failure of these organs is another common reason for seeking advice.

The diagnosis depends upon examination of the bone-marrow where the characteristic malignant plasma cells are found. X-ray films of the skull, spine, and other bones may show appearances due to destruction by the plasma cell tumours. One of the functions of the plasma cell is to make the immunoglobulins, one of the protein substances normally present in the blood. The amount of immunoglobulin in the blood can be measured and a great excess is virtually diagnostic of myelomatosis. A related protein substance is to be found in the urine in 30 per cent and is often the clue to the diagnosis.

Chemotherapy is at present the only specific treatment effective. Many combinations have been used but repeated courses of a corticosteroid with a nitrogen-mustard, melphalan, have proved the most valuable. It is a disease with a variable and unpredictable course. There are reports of survival for 20 years without specific treatment. Since the introduction of chemotherapy the median survival has increased from 7 months to between 24 and 50 months. Supportive treatment to manage the many complications of myelomatosis is important and demands much skill and experience. The use of interferon is noted in Chapter 8.

Lymphoma

The lymphomas as malignant tumours which arise from the fixed cells of the lymphoreticular tissues briefly described in the first few paragraphs of this chapter. They differ from the leukaemias in many ways. They commonly give rise to local tumours and only rarely, and then terminally, do malignant cells spill over into the blood. The tumours commonly arise in lymphatic glands and their microscopical appearances are so variable that even today no classification has proved generally acceptable. There is one type, however, which can by general agreement be recognized and separated from all other lymphomas, this is Hodgkin's disease, and makes up some 30 per cent of this group. The custom has grown up of dividing these disorders into Hodgkin's disease and others, to those others the inelegant title of 'non-Hodgkin lymphoma' is now usually applied.

Hodgkin's disease

Hodgkin's disease is not common but it has an importance out of all proportion to its frequency. Advances in its management over the last 15 years have changed the outlook for the sufferer in the early stage of this disease from one of certain death to one of almost certain recovery. It was in Hodgkin's disease that the value of combination chemotherapy first became apparent and that the necessity of precise 'staging' was established.

Hodgkin's disease is a malignant tumour believed to arise from cells called histiocytes which spring from the monocyte of the blood. The appearances under the microscope are variable and this is thought to be due to the variable reaction of the normal tissues to the presence of the tumour cells.

The incidence of the disease varies from country to country, but this probably reflects the quality of diagnostic expertise. The registered incidence in England and Wales per 1 000 000 per year for the period 1963–6 was 30 for men and 19 for women: in West Germany the figures were 38 and 28 and in Japan 6 and 3. In 1975, 456 men and 375 women were certified as dying from Hodgkin's disease in England and Wales giving mortality rates for the year of 19 and 11. In 1961 these rates were 24 and 13. These changes suggest that the advances in its treatment are beginning to have some impact.

The figures for age incidence show two peaks, one at 20 and one at 70 years, suggesting to some that there are two separated disorders. The proportion of men to women lies between 1.6 to 1 and 1.2 to 1. There are no clues to its causation, although more than one member of a family is affected more frequently than would be expected, but the same is true of husbands and wives.

Most often the patient consults his doctor because he has noticed an enlarged lymphatic gland. In over half the glandular enlargement is in the neck, in one-tenth in the armpit, and rarely in the groin. Occasionally an X-ray reveals enlarged lymphatic glands in the chest. At this stage general symptoms are rare; a few complain of lassitude, loss of weight, sweating or irritation of the skin. If not treated the disease spreads to glands in the neighbourhood of those first affected and fever, emaciation, and anaemia make their appearance. Finally, deposits occur in many organs and tissues and death takes place from exhaustion, infection, and anaemia. This course is rarely seen nowadays.

When the enlarged glands are noted one should immediately be removed for microscopic examination; only in this way can the diagnosis be made. There are four microscopic patterns of Hodgkin's disease and the pathologist will allot the gland he examines to one of these for the outlook in each differs considerably. The second stage is to determine the exact extent of the disease. This is essential to rational planning of treatment. In addition to simple physical examination it demands X-rays of the lungs, tests of the liver, lymphography (see Chapter 6), examination of the bone marrow, and finally a surgical exploration of the abdomen to make certain that there is no spread of the disease to the many lymphatic glands it contains and remove the spleen. This process of 'staging' is essential to determine the appropriate treatment. In general radiotherapy gives results superior to chemotherapy but if any area of disease is not treated relapse is inevitable. Thus radiotherapy is indicated only when it is certain that all the affected glands can be irradiated. The usual method is to include in the area treated the central region of the chest, both armpits and both sides of the neck; this is known as the 'upper mantle' field. When treatment of this area is complete, a field called the 'inverted Y' including the central strip of the abdomen and the two groins is irradiated. This method, when shown by staging to be appropriate, results in 80 per cent of patients surviving 5 years and if free from disease at that time it is justifiable to consider them cured.

Chemotherapy is employed when radiotherapy is considered inappropriate. Many drugs and schedules have been used but intermittent courses of several drugs in combination are now firmly established as the treatment of choice. The drugs commonly used are nitrogen mustard, vinblastine, procarbazine, and one of the cortisone-like agents. In one series treated in this way in whom the disease was too widespread for radiotherapy, 80 per cent of patients were alive after five years. Chemotherapy is also valuable as an adjuvant to radiotherapy.

As in most of these diseases, supportive treatment is often required and may include blood transfusion and antibiotics. There are occasional instances where removal of the spleen is valuable.

The overall outlook in this disease means little. Prognosis depends upon the microscopic type and the stage at which treatment is undertaken. When both are favourable the proportion surviving at 5 years is over 90 per cent; when the microscopic pattern is unfavourable and the disease generalized the proportion falls to about 20 per cent.

Non-Hodgkin lymphoma

This title would be inexcusable if it were not so convenient. The tumours it includes are of many microscopic patterns but all arise from cells of the lymphoreticular system. In the past they have been known as lymphosarcomas, reticulosarcomas, and reticulum cell sarcomas. In 1975, 962 men and 882 women were certified as dying from diseases which fall into this group in England and Wales. The mortality rates for this year per 1 000 000 living were 40 for males and 35 females. The non-Hodgkin lymphomas make up 69 per cent of all lymphomas.

Leukaemia and lymphoma

Pathologists have debated classification of these tumours for many years and there is as yet no general acceptance of any one plan. In the early stages they almost always declare themselves by enlargement of lymphatic glands, usually first noticed in the neck. Sometimes the early symptoms arise from enlarged glands within the abdomen. Some of these tumours are aggressive and spread rapidly; others run an indolent course, but when first seen in 75 per cent the malignant process is no longer restricted to one group of glands. The diagnosis depends upon microscopic study of an excised gland and this will also give some indication of the course the disease is likely to run. In the later stages tumour cells may escape into the blood and the picture mimics that of a leukaemia.

Non-Hodgkin lymphoma does not appear to spread in the orderly fashion shown by Hodgkin's disease and 'staging' seems to be of less value. When there is good evidence that the disease is localized radiotherapy is appropriate, but where it is generalized from the onset, as is often the case, chemotherapy is required. It is usually given as a combination of cyclophosphamide, vincristine, and a cortisone-like preparation. About 50 per cent will undergo complete remission with this treatment but relapse is almost inevitable. The duration of remission depends much upon the microscopic type of the tumour, but the lack of an agreed classification makes comparison between the results of different centres impossible. In one series the period for which 50 per cent of the patients survived varied with the different microscopic types from 1 year to 8 years.

A brief mention must be made of Burkitt's lymphoma, a malignant tumour of lymphocytes occurring almost exclusively in native children in Africa and New Guinea. It is closely associated with the Epstein–Barr virus (see Chapter 2) which has been incriminated as the cause of glandular fever and is also associated with nasopharyngeal carcinoma. Its possible role in the cause of both Burkitt's lymphoma and nasopharyngeal cancer is undecided.

177

Cancer – the facts

It usually presents as a tumour of the jaw. It is uniquely sensitive to cyclophosphamide, one dose of which will lead to complete remission in over half these children. With maintenance treatment a high proportion are cured, but if this is neglected the tumour becomes generalized.

15

Tumours of the central nervous system

Tumours of the central nervous system are common, but exact analysis of their frequency and type is difficult because of the limits imposed by certification. In 1975 in England and Wales 1077 men and 771 women were certified as dying from 'malignant neoplasm of the brain', giving mortality rates for the year of 45 and 31 per 1 000 000 living. The figures for deaths from all neoplasms of the brain and nervous system for that year were 1546 men and 1261 women with mortality rates of 64 and 50. There has been a considerable increase in deaths from this cause over the last 35 years: for 1941–45 the yearly mortality rates averaged 23 for men and 15 for women, by the quinquennium 1966–70 they had increased to 49 and 33. Tumours of the nervous system account for a little over 2 per cent of all deaths from cancer.

Many classifications of tumours of the nervous system have been devised, but none is universally accepted except in broad outlines. About half the tumours arise in the substance of the brain itself or less commonly in that of the spinal cord. They originate from the cells of the supporting tissue of the nervous system which is known as the neuroglia and is comparable with the connective tissue in other parts of the body. These tumours are called gliomas and they are malignant in the sense that they invade and infiltrate the neighbouring parts of the brain leaving no clear demarcation between the tumour and the normal brain substance. However they never give rise to metastases. There are several different types: at one end of the scale is the slowly growing 'astrocytoma' and at the other the rapidly advancing invasive 'glioblastoma'. The first, not uncommon in children and accounting for one-quarter of gliomas, carries a mean survival of 8 years. The second makes up about half of all gliomas, occurs usually between 40 and 60 years of age and commonly leads to death in 12 months. Another glioma which pursues a rapid course if not treated is the medulloblastoma usually seen before the age of 10 years. It has the unusual property of causing metastases elsewhere in the central nervous system by shedding its cells into the cerebrospinal fluid which bathes the brain and spinal cord.

The other common tumours are those arising from the meninges, the membranes which enclose the brain and the spinal cord. Called meningiomas, they amount to about one-fifth of all growths of the nervous system. They are almost always benign in that they do not infiltrate nor give rise to metastases, but cause symptoms by pressure on the brain or spinal cord. There are a number of rarer primary forms which do not merit discussion in this book, but probably a quarter of all brain tumours are metastases, secondary deposits from cancers elsewhere in the body. Mention has already been made (see Chapter 7) of the frequency with which cancer of the lung gives rise to cerebral metastases: other common primary tumours which often lead to second-ary deposits in the brain are cancers of the breast and the large bowel.

Tumours of the brain may occur at any age, but they are common below the age of 10 years and there is another peak in their incidence between the ages of 50 and 70. They are somewhat more common in males than in females. There is no recognized racial predilection, although the skills needed for their diagnosis are less likely to be available in the under-developed countries.

They cause their symptoms in two ways. First, the growth may compress, irritate, or destroy the area of the brain where it arises. This will interfere with the functions for which this particular region is responsible: it may lead to weakness of one side of the body, to partial loss of sight, to disturbance of feeling in some area, to deafness, or to a host of other disabilities. As the tumour grows so will the symptoms, which usually start insidiously, gradually advance. If the tumour causes irritation of the brain tissue it may lead to epileptic fits and these are early symptoms in perhaps one-third of all those with brain tumours.

The second way in which symptoms are caused results from the tumour growing within the rigid confines of the skull. As its bulk increases so will the pressure inside the skull rise and lead to a group of characteristic symptoms. Headache is a constant feature: at first it is usually at its worst in the morning, wearing off after a few hours, later it becomes constant. It is often associated with vomiting occurring especially when the headache is most severe. Mental symptoms include loss of memory, hallucinations, and sometimes a general deterioration of intellect. If the pressure is not reduced drowsiness followed by coma and eventually death result.

Tumours of the spinal cord are rare compared with those of the brain. They exert pressure upon the cord itself which causes paralysis of the legs, with loss of feeling and often difficulty in passing water.

The diagnosis of brain tumour is founded upon a consideration of the symptoms and the results of careful examination of the nervous system. A number of instrumental aids are available; perhaps the most valuable of all and one which may well displace all others is computerized axial tomography discussed in Chapter 6. At present the cost of the apparatus prevents it being universally available, and other techniques are required. The electroencephalogram may give some information but is often of little help; isotopic scanning will reveal some but not all tumours and 'echo scanning' will show whether a tumour is displacing the brain to one side. Far and away the most useful is arteriography when an agent, opaque to X-rays, is injected into the main artery to the brain on the side suspected of having a tumour. A series of X-ray films is taken immediately and the arteries in the brain are outlined. A tumour will cause alterations in the normal anatomical arrangement of these blood vessels and can often be precisely localized (see Plate 1b).

Cancer – the facts

When a firm diagnosis of tumour of the brain has been established treatment depends upon its nature. First it is essential to exclude the possibility of it being metastatic by making as certain as possible there is no primary cancer of which it might be a secondary deposit. If there is good evidence that it is a meningioma, surgical exploration should be undertaken at once. These are benign tumours and can usually be removed completely; they cause their symptoms by compressing the brain tissue and if this is allowed to continue the damage may become irreversible. If the tumour proves to be within the substance of the brain it is almost certainly a glioma. It is likely to be impossible to remove it completely, but many neurosurgeons feel that a biopsy should be made and this can usually be carried out with a needle through a small hole drilled through the skull. The patient can often be helped by partial removal of a glioma. The site of the tumour determines whether this is feasible or indeed justifiable; injudicious operation will result in unacceptable disability. With a rapidly progressive glioma, partial removal followed by radiotherapy increases survival from about 6 months to between 18 and 24 months. In the case of a glioma of low malignancy early operation carries a mortality of 5 per cent and after radiotherapy recurrence may not occur for 10 years or longer. If surgery is deferred until there are signs of a raised pressure within the skull the operative mortality rises to 15–20 per cent and recurrence is likely within 2 or 3 years. Glioma therefore is best managed by partial removal of the tumour except in the rare instances when it is possible to excise it completely. Operation is followed by radiotherapy to which gliomas vary in their responsiveness. The medulloblastoma is extremely sensitive and when treated in the way outlined above the average survival at 5 years is 30 per cent; there is however little likelihood of cure. The glioblastoma is moderately sensitive; the astrocytoma shows little response, but remains the glioma with the best outlook.

If a decision is taken that operation is unjustifiable, efforts must be made to reduce the pressure within the skull. The most effective method of achieving this and relieving the patient's discomfort is by giving a cortisone-like preparation – dexamethasone. Its effects are often surprisingly dramatic.

When the tumour is metastatic heroic treatment has no place. In most there will prove to be more than one secondary deposit. It is almost impossible to be certain that it is solitary, and assuming the primary tumour had been 'cured', only then would removal be justified. Chemotherapy may often bring about temporary improvement and dexamethasone is as valuable in patients with secondary as in those with primary tumours.

It should be noted that tumours which exert pressure on the spinal cord most commonly arise by spread from secondary deposits of cancer in the bones of the spine. X-ray examination will confirm or exclude this cause. When a primary spinal tumour seems likely the diagnosis is established by injecting a radio-opaque fluid into the subarachnoid space which surrounds the spinal cord and through which the cerebrospinal fluid circulates. X-ray films will show where the dye is arrested and will outline the tumour. Surgical exploration should then be undertaken, for most of these tumours are benign and can be removed with complete and permanent restoration of function. If it proves to be malignant and removal is impossible radiotherapy remains the only available treatment.

16

Cancer of the skin

Cancers of the skin are common; they may be primary or secondary. The latter occur perhaps most frequently in those with cancer of the breast when, apart from direct invasion by an underlying growth, small nodules in the skin are often seen. There are a number of rare primary tumours but only two of importance: carcinoma and melanoma.

Cancer of the skin

This is perhaps the commonest of all malignant diseases. It is seldom fatal. In England and Wales in 1975, 235 men and 242 women were certified as dying from this disease: the mortality rates per 1 000 000 living were 10 for each sex. These figures contrast strongly with the overall numbers per 1 000 000 registered per year for the period 1963–6 which were 340 men and 267 women.

The disease is more common in the elderly and in those of fair skin constantly exposed to sunlight. It occurs after exposure to ionizing radiation and there are a number of chemical agents which appear to have induced it (Chapter 2). It is far more often seen in the white races than in the dark-skinned and there are a number of skin disorders which must be regarded as precancerous.

Two pathological types are recognized. The first and most common is the basal-cell carcinoma often called the rodent ulcer. It arises from cells in the deeper layers of the skin. It is slow growing and never metastasizes nor spreads to the regional lymphatic glands. Indeed, it can be regarded as only 'locally malignant'. The second type, the squamous cell carcinoma, originates from cells of the more superficial layers of the skin. It spreads to the regional lymphatic glands in about 10 per cent, but seldom if ever gives rise to distant metastases. It occasionally arises in a long-standing ulcer and sometimes in scars.

There is rarely any difficulty in diagnosis. The rodent ulcer occurs most often on the face. Both advance slowly leading to an ulcer with thickened rolled edges. If neglected the tumours invade and destroy the deeper tissues. Diagnosis must be confirmed by biopsy.

In rodent ulcer, local excision or irradiation results in cure in 100 per cent. The squamous cell variety requires rather wider excision and if there is any enlargement of lymphatic glands these also need to be removed and operation is often followed by radiotherapy.

When there is no enlargement of lymphatic glands operation is curative in 95 per cent of patients; when enlarged glands require removal the proportion falls to 70 per cent. When there is recurrence after surgery or radiotherapy it drops still further to 50 per cent.

Malignant melanomas

Malignant melanoma is a cancer derived from melanocytes. These cells lie in the deeper layers of the skin and their function is to form the dark pigment which develops when the skin is exposed to the sun. It is a rare disease, but a rapidly progressive one. In 1975, 282 men and 370 women were certified as dying from malignant melanoma in England and Wales, giving mortality rates of 12 and 15 per 1 000 000 living. It is responsible for 0.5 per cent of all deaths from cancer. There are few clues to its cause, although it is commoner in those of fair skin who are constantly exposed to sunlight. In England and Wales the number per 1 000 000 living registered per year as having malignant melanomas were 13 men and 25 women. In the State of Queensland the total registrations amount to 160 per 1 000 000 living per year. It is rare in dark-skinned races and in childhood. It commonly makes its appearance between the ages of 40 and 70 years.

It is generally believed that most malignant melanomas begin in moles. These are extremely common and the melanoma is rare: the chances of an ordinary mole becoming malignant are said to be 1 in 1 000 000. Suspicions that this change had taken place would be aroused by an increase in size of the mole, bleeding from its surface, and the sensation that it was fixed to the tissues underneath it. However the cancer arises it spreads rapidly, soon invading the lymphatic glands in the region and giving rise early to metastases, especially in the lungs, liver, and brain. Its behaviour is often bizarre: the primary tumour may disappear completely leaving enlarged lymphatic glands in which the cancer makes rapid progress. At other times an enlarged gland is found which biopsy proves to be infiltrated by malignant melanoma and no sign of a primary cancer can be discovered. Diagnosis is seldom difficult, but a suspicious mole must always be removed and if microscopic examination shows it to be malignant a more extensive operation undertaken without delay.

At present surgery offers the only hope of cure and the excision must be wide and deep. Unsightly scars may result but a radical operation is essential and it may be necessary to graft skin over the area.

'Regional chemotherapy' has been widely used in malignant melanoma. The anticancer drug is injected continuously by a 'drip' method for a few hours into the artery which supplies blood to the limb bearing the tumour. The results are not impressive. The tumours show little response to radiotherapy.

The outlook is better in women than in men and least favourable with tumours situated on the head, the upper part of the arm, and the leg. Overall the proportion surviving at 5 years is 50 per cent and at 10 years 30 per cent. If there has been no spread to the glands the 5-year survival is 50–60 per cent, but if the regional glands have been invaded it falls to 15 per cent.

17

Cancer of the endocrine glands

Cancers of the endocrine organs or glands of internal secretion are uncommon, but of some theoretical interest for they are often associated with overactivity of the affected gland. Most are of such rarity that comment would be inappropriate in a book of this kind; those of the thyroid and the suprarenal glands alone deserve consideration.

Cancers of the thyroid gland

The thyroid gland lies in the neck just below the larynx athwart the upper end of the windpipe. Malignant disease arising in this organ was the certified cause of death in 114 men and 292 women in England and Wales in 1975. The mortality rates were 5 and 12 for the two sexes and the disease was responsible for 0.2 per cent of male deaths from cancer and 0.5 per cent of female. The mortality rates per year for the period 1931–5 were 3 for men and 9 for women. Thus there has been some increase in the numbers dying of thyroid cancer and this is particularly evident in the younger age groups. The registered rates of incidence per million living per year for 1963–6 were 7 for males and 18 for women, and comparison with the mortality rates of 4 and 12 shows it to carry a reasonably good outlook.

Overall, females are affected nearly three times more often than males, but below the age of 12 years the ratio is 1:1. There are minor peaks in the curve of incidence between 7 and 20 years and again between 40 and 65 years. In those countries where distance from the sea results in deficiency of iodine and leads to the enlargement of the thyroid known as goitre, cancer of the gland is more common, particularly in men. Thus in Switzerland the mortality rate for 1965 was 12 for men and 14 for women compared with 4 and 12 in

England and Wales. It is said that the general use of iodine added to salt or to the water supply has some protective effect. The other causal factor of importance is ionizing radiation. A history of such exposure can be obtained in 30–40 per cent of children with cancer of the thyroid. The average interval between irradiation and the appearance of malignant change is 9 years.

A number of forms of malignant disease may affect the thyroid gland. The majority are carcinomas arising from the glandular cells and they fall into two main groups: one slow growing and indolent, the other aggressive and of rapid growth. The microscopic patterns of the first are recognized. One, because the cells are arranged in a manner resembling the fronds of a fern, is known as 'papillary'; in the second, the follicular type, the appearances closely mimic those of the normal gland. Sixty per cent of thyroid cancers are of the papillary type and this is the common variety in children. They spread early to the neighbouring lymphatic glands. Twenty-five per cent are follicular; this type occurs in middle age and seldom spreads to the lymphatic glands, but leads to metastases, especially in the lungs and bone. It is sometimes responsible for the symptoms of thyroid overactivity. The remainder are of the aggressive, rapidly advancing variety. It tends to occur in the elderly and spreads to infiltrate the neighbouring tissues.

The first sign of cancer of the thyroid is usually a lump lying in the gland itself. The papillary cancers often spread to lymphatic glands before themselves causing a swelling large enough to be felt. Sometimes the tumour has all the features of a malignant growth, being anchored to the deeper tissues, causing difficulty in swallowing, and possibly also of breathing. If there is any doubt biopsy must be carried out at once.

Isotopic scanning with radioactive iodine (see Chapter 2) may be useful. Most cancers are 'cold' and do not take up the isotope. Indeed it is usual to advise removal of any 'cold' thyroid swelling. The activity of some thyroid tumours is

Cancers of the endocrine glands

increased by the thyroid stimulating hormones of the pituitary gland. They are in this sense 'hormone dependent' and give a positive result with the scan. The same is true of their metastases which can be localized by this method. About 15 per cent of papillary growths and a higher proportion of follicular have this property.

Treatment consists of surgical removal of the thyroid gland and of the neighbouring lymphatic glands if they are thought to be diseased. It is often worth excising any solitary metastasis when this is technically possible. The tumours which take up radioactive iodine are often responsive to the thyroid hormone thyroxine which in this respect is antagonistic to the thyroid-stimulating hormone on which they are dependent. Metastases, especially in the lungs, can often be controlled by this means for years. Radiotherapy is usually reserved for the aggressive growths where radical operation is impossible. Chemotherapy has little value in this disease.

With the exception of the aggressive type, cancer of the thyroid is the most chronic of all malignant diseases. The outlook depends upon the type of growth and upon the age and sex of the patient. Women fare better than men and children better than the elderly. In the papillary variety the survival at 10 years after treatment averages 80 per cent; in the follicular 60 per cent; but in the aggressive type of growth not more than 1 per cent.

Cancers of the suprarenal glands

The two suprarenal glands rest one upon the upper part of each kidney. Each is in reality two different glands having an inner core or medulla which secretes the hormone adrenalin, and an outer covering or cortex responsible for the formation of cortisone-like and some sex hormones. Cancers of the glands are of great rarity and accounted for only 48 deaths in England and Wales in 1975 or 1 per 1 000 000 living.

A cancer of the cortex of the gland leads to excessive production of hormones resulting in obesity, overgrowth of hair, a raised blood pressure, and easy bruising. Sometimes women develop masculine characteristics and men feminine. The treatment is surgical removal. It is of interest that there is a drug, mutotane, which has a direct destructive effect upon the cells of this cancer. Unfortunately, it also carries a number of undesirable side effects which greatly limit its value.

The medulla of the suprarenal is the origin of one of the commonest cancers of childhood, called the neuroblastoma. This occurs before the age of 5 years, and causes a massive abdominal tumour. It spreads rapidly, having a particular tendency to metastasize in bones. Early operation offers the only choice of cure.

The other cancer which may arise in the medulla of the suprarenal is one which leads to overproduction of adrenalin with attacks in which there is shaking, sweating, and a brisk rise in blood pressure, often to high levels. It is known as phaeochromocytoma. This tumour is usually benign but in one-tenth of cases it is cancerous. The treatment is surgical removal.

18

Cancer of bones and soft tissues

Primary cancers of bone

These are uncommon and considerably more rare than secondary deposits from tumours arising in such organs as the breast, the lung, the thyroid, and the kidney. In 1975, 244 men and 197 women were certified as dying from 'malignant neoplasms of bone' in England and Wales. The mortality rates per 1 000 000 living for that year were 10 and 8. It is reasonable to assume the majority of these deaths were due to primary bone cancers. Males are affected rather more frequently than females and there is a peak in the curve of incidence between the ages of 15 and 24 years, although the majority of deaths are in the elderly.

There are several different kinds of malignant tumour of bone and they have been divided into those which arise from cells engaged in forming or absorbing bone and those which originate from other types of cell. They fall into the pathological class of sarcoma. The first category contains three varieties of importance: the osteosarcoma, the chondrosarcoma, and the giant-cell tumour. The second has one important type, known as Ewing's tumour, but various cancers arising in cells of the bone marrow such as lymphomas and myelomas (Chapter 14), in spite of their origins, are often classed as primary bone tumours.

Osteosarcoma

Osteosarcoma makes up about 40 per cent of primary bone cancers. It is seen most often in males – the proportion being 3:2 – and between the age of 10 and 20 years. The majority arise in the upper ends of the thigh bone, the tibia, or the humerus. The usual complaint is of a painful tender swelling. The diagnosis is usually possible from the appearances in

191

an X-ray film, but always needs to be confirmed by biopsy. Blood-borne metastases occur soon and especially in the lungs: without early treatment they usually appear within 6–9 months. The lymphatic glands are rarely affected. If there has been no spread of the disease amputation of the affected limb is the accepted treatment. Some believe that irradiation of the tumour before operation increases the number of recoveries. Post-operative radiotherapy has been the rule, but of late years chemotherapy with various drug combinations has been found effective in preventing, or at worst postponing, metastases. It is not certain yet how its results compare with those of radiotherapy. At present the overall survival at 5 years is 20 per cent and at 10 years 17 per cent.

Chondrosarcoma

The chondrosarcoma originates from cells which give rise to cartilage and makes up 10 per cent of primary bone cancers. It is most common in men aged 50–60 years. The bones from which it most frequently arises are those of the pelvis, the ribs, and the femur. It is a slow-growing tumour which causes little pain and only leads to metastases late. Amputation or surgical removal where possible is the usual treatment. It is resistant to radiotherapy and chemotherapy.

The origin of Ewing tumour is still uncertain – some regard it as a lymphoma, but this view is not generally accepted. It makes up 12 per cent of primary bone tumours. It arises in long bones most often between the ages of 10 and 20 years and 60 per cent of the patients are male. It is an aggressive form of cancer which leads early to metastases: indeed secondary deposits are present in at least one-fifth when advice is first sought. Until recently the results of treatment have been depressing: the overall 5-year survival hitherto has been only 8 per cent. There is no general agreement on whether amputation followed by radiotherapy is more effective than radiotherapy alone. During the past few years chemotherapy combined with radiotherapy has given encouraging results in one small series. Twelve patients thus treated were all well after 40 months, whereas of 18 treated by radiotherapy and surgery only 1 survived.

Cancers of the soft tissues

Cancers of soft tissues include those arising in muscle, fat, and the supporting or connective tissues other than bone. They also fall into the class of 'sarcoma'. The name of each tumour is usually qualified by a prefix indicating its origin. Soft tissue sarcomas are rare. In 1975 the numbers certified as dying from such neoplasms in England and Wales was 169 men and 153 women. The mortality rates per 1 000 000 living for the year were 7 and 6.

There is a suggestion that viral infection may play some part in their cause, but, as usual when this suggestion is made, firm evidence is lacking. Although rare, some fifty varieties of soft tissue sarcomas have been described. Over one-half is made up of three types – 23 per cent are liposarcomas, arising from fat cells, 21 per cent are fibrosarcomas, derived from fibrous tissue, and 10 per cent rhabdomyosarcomas from muscles. They usually start as swellings which are not as a rule painful. Radical excision is the accepted form of treatment when possible. The sensitivity of these tumours to radiotherapy varies with the type and the same is true of chemotherapy. They are usually slow growing, giving rise to metastases late, and rarely spreading to lymphatic glands. The overall proportions surviving at 5 and 10 years for the three most common varieties are: liposarcoma 60 per cent and 56 per cent; fibrosarcoma 77 per cent and 71 per cent; and rhabdomyosarcoma 60 per cent and 45 per cent. Chemotherapy has given impressive results in this last tumour: treatment with combinations of drugs following surgery have yielded a 2-year survival of 75 per cent in those whose outlook was accounted poor. It is likely that this form of treatment will make unnecessary the extensive and mutilating operations now deemed advisable.

19

Retrospect and prospect

To many without a background of training in science the word 'research' has a romantic ring suggesting what the lay press is pleased to call 'a break-through'. The truth is quite different. Scientific research rarely depends upon the sudden intuitive flash of genius, much more often it is based on meticulous, plodding, and dull routine with the occasional leaven of a lucky guess. It is this which slowly extends the boundaries of scientific knowledge and in no field is it more true than in that of cancer research. Many believe that discovery of the 'cause of cancer' is around the corner, but those who have read the earlier chapters of this book will appreciate that to speak of the 'cause of cancer' is meaningless. The very nature of malignant disease is ill-understood, but in many instances causes can be recognized which will pull the trigger starting the mysterious process we know as cancer. Knowledge and understanding of the nature of the malignant process is clearly desirable, but it would be naive to assume that their acquisition would immediately provide a cure for the many diseases falling under the head of cancer.

Innumerable research institutions are engaged in seeking answers to the many questions posed by malignant disease. Much of this research is aimed at solving such basic problems as the nature of the change responsible for the disorderly growth which stamps a cell as malignant. The molecular biology of tumours, the part played by viruses and the genetic, immunological, and experimental aspects of tumour growth are the subjects of study in centres throughout the world. To the layman the relevance of much of this laborious and painstaking work may seem remote. To him the research which matters is that which leads to cure. Nevertheless, the importance of these fundamental enquiries cannot be overestimated.

194

Retrospect and prospect

Ultimate control of cancer cannot be envisaged without a clear understanding of the malignant process and knowledge of the factors which initiate it.

Pari passu with these basic researches, practising doctors are constantly seeking methods by which cancer may be prevented, recognized at an earlier stage, and treated more effectively. It is such research, having an immediate and practical application, that is more likely to be the concern of those who read this book. In this chapter the advances of the past 30 or 40 years are briefly reviewed, for by projection into the future they may give some indication of what progress may be expected.

Before considering the purely technical advances it is wise to examine changes during the past few years in the care of the patient with cancer. Formerly he usually found himself referred to a physician or surgeon whose interest lay in disease of the organ or tissue from which the growth arose. Thus a patient with cancer of the stomach would be treated by a surgeon expert in operations on that organ, or one with cancer of the lung by a chest surgeon. Once the necessary surgery was completed, interest was likely to wane for the surgeon's training ensures that he will be more concerned with the technical problems of operative surgery than with those of malignant disease. It might be that radiotherapy was necessary and the patient would then be transferred to the care of the radiotherapist. Continuity and co-operation were often lacking. It was barely appreciated that the patient with cancer presented special problems, both physical and psychological, irrespective of the organ from which the malignant tumour arose. In many centres now there are departments of oncology in which the interest is focused on the total management of the patient with cancer.

It is now generally appreciated that better results are obtained when from the beginning there is co-operation between the medical oncologist, the surgeon, and the radiotherapist. Treatment is no longer by rule of thumb, it is carefully planned after consultation between these three and the patient's subsequent course is closely supervized. Such co-operation results not only in better treatment, but provides the patient with the support which was often lacking in the past. Continuity of care and ready availability are of the first importance and may be difficult for surgeon or radiotherapist to provide for both are in essence experts in the application of specific forms of treatment. Without these the patient cannot feel secure and will not know to whom he can turn. The notion of the oncological team able to provide this continuity is a new one, but its wider adoption will greatly improve the lot of the sufferer from cancer.

The kind of result which such co-operation can achieve is shown by a recently published case report of which the following is a resumé. It highlights the fortitude demanded of the patient no less than the expertise displayed by the oncological team.

A 25-year-old man was found to have a tumour of the right testicle which on removal proved to be a teratoma. A lymphogram showed the disease to have spread to the lymphatic glands within the abdomen and these were treated with a full course of radiotherapy.

A year later he complained of severe headache and a partial paralysis of the left side of his body became evident. At the same time he developed what appeared to be pneumonia of the lower part of the right lung. X-ray films of the chest showed him to have isolated metastases in both the right and the left lung. A computerized axial tomogram disclosed a metastasis in the right side of the brain. A further lymphogram showed the enlarged lymphatic glands in the abdomen had disappeared.

Over the next 12 months he was given 19 courses of chemotherapy in which combinations of 10 different drugs were used together with injections into the subarachnoid space.

Significant improvement followed this treatment and operations were carried out to remove the metastatic residues first from the right, then from the left lung. These were succeeded by another two months of chemotherapy before an operation to remove the metastasis from the brain was undertaken. Thereafter he received 21 radiotherapeutic treatments to the brain combined with 10 injections of anticancer drugs into the subarachnoid space.

All treatment was stopped 15 months ago, he has remained well without any sign of disease and has resumed work. The only ill-effects of his treatment are some baldness, occasional loss of memory, and some impairment of hearing.

Retrospect and prospect

An important advance during the last ten years has been in the care of those in whom the disease has escaped from control. There has been a gradual realization of the many problems, psychological and physical, which incurable cancer brings. Again, this is a recent development, but there are now a number of centres in this country which provide this invaluable service. Medical and nursing staff in these centres or hospices have dedicated themselves to the care of those with advanced malignant disease who cannot be managed at home. Careful studies have been made of how to control symptoms and how best to use pain-killing drugs. Great expertise has been developed in the relief of physical discomfort. As important is the ability of the staff to establish the psychological rapport with the patients which allows free discussion of their fears and anxieties. No-one who has visited a hospice of this kind can fail to be impressed by the peace and serenity with which it endows the closing days of the sufferer from cancer.

Prevention of malignant disease should ideally take precedence over treatment. The subject has been discussed in Chapter 7. The notion of the external or environmental cause of cancer sprang from Percival Pott's observations 200 years ago on cancer of the scrotum in chimney sweeps. It was the foundation of cancer epidemiology, although the scientific study of geographical variations in the incidence of the various forms of malignant disease dates back only to the beginning of this century. Nevertheless, it has yielded a rich harvest, bringing to light innumerable occupational and environmental causes of cancer. Indeed cancer epidemiologists are convinced that at least 80 per cent of all types of malignant disease will eventually prove to be of environmental origin. Similarly the relatively rare varieties in which genetic factors are of importance have been carefully studied and the patterns of inheritance established.

It is clearly possible to prevent environmental forms of cancer, provided that the carcinogen can be controlled and that advice be accepted. Both these provisos are difficult to observe. When the carcinogen is of occupational origin, such as exposure to asbestos, control can be imposed by statute; where exposure is voluntary, as in the case of cigarette smoke, experience has shown it to be much more difficult. Undoubtedly the next few years will see the identification of further carcinogens, but the pattern is likely to be repeated and where their control demands voluntary effort it is unlikely to be forthcoming. Similarly counselling is readily available where the possibility of genetically-determined cancer exists, but it is rarely sought and still more rarely is the advice accepted.

Prevention demands too the early detection of precancerous states and their effective treatment. More and more of these are now recognized and it seems probable that their numbers will increase still further and the need for earlier treatment will be more generally appreciated.

In the field of diagnosis almost all the instrumental and technical aids have been developed during this century: they have been discussed in detail in Chapter 6. They have led to the much earlier detection of cancer and thus in many instances to earlier treatment and greater chances of cure. Computerized axial tomography with the EMI scanner, mammography, fibre-optic endoscopy, and exfoliative cytology are a few of the technical advances of the past twenty-five years. The possibilities of many of these methods have not been fully exploited and, although they are prodigal of medical manpower and of money, it seems likely that further developments can be anticipated. Indeed provided the appropriate methods are applied the diagnosis of cancer of almost every organ in the very earliest stage is possible. Unfortunately symptoms which lead to advice being sought seldom arise at this stage. Moreover those with cancer often postpone consulting the doctor until symptoms have been present for months or have become intolerable. This will be remedied only by a wider knowledge of malignant disease and the appreciation that cure usually depends on early diagnosis and early treatment. The alternative would be universal screening, but this demands voluntary co-operation and is so expensive that it is clearly only justifiable in common types of cancer and when it is technically simple. Cancer of the cervix and of the breast are the two prime examples and are discussed in Chapter 7. There can be little doubt that the next few years will see a great extension of the facilities for screening for both these tumours, but at present expense will prevent the inclusion of other cancers.

It is naturally in the realm of treatment that there is most interest. Surgery remains pre-eminent although, as often said, it must be considered a tacit admission of failure. Nevertheless the technical expertise of the surgeon is something for which innumerable sufferers from cancer are grateful. His ability to carry out more extensive and more radical operations has increased greatly in recent years. This is not to be attributed to an increase in his skill, which has always been of a high order. It is due to advances in anaesthesia, the control of infections by antibiotics, the use of blood transfusions, and to immensely improved post-operative management. Surgery appears to have reached the pinnacle of achievement and it is difficult to see what major advances there can be in the surgical treatment of cancer. Nevertheless at various times over the past 100 years this opinion has been expressed by those astonished alike by the technical ability of the surgeon and by the capacity of the human body to withstand his onslaught, and has been proved wrong.

The second line of treatment is radiotherapy and it is only as old as the century. In that time immense advances have been made culminating in supervoltage therapy. The last thirty years have seen the development of radioactive isotopes in treatment, but it is true to say that they have proved less valuable than anticipated. Indeed they are little used except as radioactive phosphorus in the treatment of polycythaemia vera and radioactive iodine in the treatment of some forms of cancer of the thyroid gland. It is not easy to foresee further technical advances in radiotherapy, for it has reached a high degree of efficiency. The number of malignant tumours curable by radiotherapy alone is small. Cancers of the skin, lips, and larynx are examples and the wide field irradiation of patients with Hodgkin's disease is a notable advance. Developments are much more likely in the form of combinations with surgery and chemotherapy. It remains too an invaluable palliative in controlling pain, especially from secondary deposits in bone.

Chemotherapy is the latest addition to the effective forms of treatment of malignant disease. Radiotherapy damages healthy and cancer cells alike and chemotherapy has the same limitations in that no drug has been found which will kill cancer cells without injuring healthy ones (Chapter 8). Nevertheless malignant cells are often rather more sensitive to and recover rather less rapidly from the effect of anticancer drugs than do their healthy counterparts. The first trials of cancer chemotherapy took place during World War II and its development is described in Chapter 8. At present its successes are few, but it has cured patients with acute leukaemia, Hodgkin's disease, and choriocarcinoma. In conjunction with radiotherapy and surgery it has greatly improved the outlook in those with several rare tumours such as nephroblastoma, rhabdomyosarcoma, and Ewing's tumour of bone. It has prolonged the survival of those with cancers of the breast and ovary. The results obtained have been greatly improved since the introduction of combinations of drugs given at intervals long enough to allow the normal healthy tissues to recover.

Many feel that chemotherapy holds great hope for the future. It is here that basic research may have an immediate practical application. At present no differences have been detected between the vital processes which take place within the cancer cell and those of the healthy cell. It seems certain that some must exist and if they can be identified it should be possible to devise drugs which would disrupt those of the cancer cell without affecting those of healthy tissue. This would provide the long-awaited specific anticancer drug. Meanwhile new drugs with anticancer activity are constantly being synthesized and submitted to trial; and experiments with different combinations of drugs and different intervals between doses continue.

Treatment with hormones has proved effective in one or two specific types of cancer. Its value in cancer of the breast, the body of the uterus, the prostate, and the thyroid gland has been described, but it is difficult to see that it can have wider applications. No other tumours have proved 'hormone dependent' and it seems unlikely that further advances will take place in this direction.

Immunotherapy has proved disappointing. Early observations suggested that the survival of patients with acute leukaemia could be prolonged by such means, but they have not been confirmed. It appears that antibodies which were thought at first to be directed specifically against cancer cells are in fact quite non-specific and cannot be shown to exert any curative effect. Immunotherapy as a form of treatment for cancer holds little promise for the future.

It has become a routine in most large centres to follow the fate of all those treated for cancer. The results of treatment are constantly reviewed, analysed, and compared with those achieved by other centres. Conferences, both national and international, are held at frequent intervals, results are reported, and new methods of treatment are described. It is true to say that the general principles of treating all forms of malignant disease are the same in all the developed countries and that there is such free international intercommunication that every worker in this field is familiar, or can easily make himself familiar, with the methods and results of every other worker. The treatment recommended by the leading centres will be the same whether advice is sought in London, Paris, Boston, or Geneva, or in Munich, Stockholm, Amsterdam, or Sydney.

It is notoriously dangerous to try and predict the pattern of future developments. This brief review will show how much has been achieved even in the last thirty years and it is likely that progress along similar lines will continue. Perhaps

201

Cancer – the facts

the most important advance has been in the use of drugs in the treatment of cancer. Forty years ago the very notion that malignant disease could be cured or even influenced by drugs would have been derided, but it is now generally agreed that it is in this field that advances in treatment are likely to occur. Nevertheless until more is known of the vital changes within the cell that lead to the disorder of growth we call cancer, the chemotherapy of this disease will continue on the hit-or-miss basis.

While search for cure continues, improvements in the care of those with cancer whether curable or not have made the lot of the patient easier to bear. The emotional impact of the disease and of the fears and anxieties the diagnosis arouses are now more widely appreciated. It is recognized that they can only be offset by knowledge and explanation. Only when the patient can talk freely and without embarrassment to his doctor and when his doctor is able to listen with patience, sympathy, and understanding, can such knowledge and explanation be provided.

Glossary

Most of the technical terms which may not be familiar to readers are defined in the text. The following glossary contains some of those which are used frequently and may present difficulties.

accelerator, linear: a machine used for radiotherapy in which a stream of electrons is accelerated by an electromagnetic wave passing down a straight tube to strike a target generating high-energy X-rays.

adenocarcinoma (*see also* carcinoma): a cancer arising from glandular cells.

aflatoxins: a group of poisonous substances produced when various moulds contaminate foodstuffs, especially maize. They have been shown to be capable of causing cancer of the liver in animals.

age-adjusted: *see* incidence and mortality.

angiography: *see* arteriography.

antibody: a specific substance produced by the body when invaded by microbes, exposed to their products, or to other proteins which are not a normal body constituent. They are capable of reacting against the causative agent and giving protection against its effects.

arteriography: a method of displaying the vessels radiographically by injecting into an artery a substance opaque to X-rays and taking immediate X-ray photographs of the area to which the artery supplies blood.

benign: of tumours; innocent as contrasted with malignant; without the features characteristic of malignant growth.

bile-duct: the duct through which the bile formed in the liver flows into the small bowel.

biopsy: removal of a fragment of tissue from the living patient for microscopical examination. It may be carried out by surgical operation or by puncture with a needle.

bronchus: the tubes springing from the wind-pipe (trachea) through which air is drawn into and expelled from the lungs.

CAT: computerized axial tomography by the EMI scanner (see page 50).

cachexia: a state of wasting, weakness, malnutrition, and anaemia characteristic of the final stages of incurable and widespread cancer.

carcinogen: an agent capable of causing cancer.

carcinoma: a cancer arising from the epithelial cells. Often qualified by an adjective denoting the type of cell from which it springs e.g. squamous, basal cell.

carcinoma-in-situ: a localized cancer in which the cells show the appearances of malignancy, but there is no infiltration, no invasion of healthy tissues, and no metastatic spread.

cell: the basic building blocks from which all living tissues are constructed. They are capable at some stage of their existence of reproduction by division. Each contains a nucleus, is surrounded by cytoplasm and bounded by a cell-membrane. They undergo development acquiring special characteristics which fit them for the specialized tasks for which they are destined. This process is called differentiation.

cerebrospinal fluid: a clear colourless fluid circulating through the subarachnoid space (q.v.) and the hollow spaces (ventricles) within the brain.

cervix: the cervix uteri. The neck of the womb; the narrow muscular tube connecting the vagina to the body of the womb (corpus uteri).

chemotherapy: treatment with pure chemical substances, usually of synthetic origin; especially applied to the treatment of cancer and infections.

chromosomes: paired bodies which carry the genes (q.v.) and are present in the nucleus of every cell. There are 24 pairs in man.

contrast-medium: a substance opaque to X-rays used to delineate a hollow structure not otherwise apparent in X-ray photographs. The barium meal is a familiar example.

cyclotron: an electromagnetic machine used for radiotherapy capable of generating a stream of electrons and of producing radioactive isotopes.

cyst: a defined cavity containing fluid.

diathermy: the use of an electrode heated by a high-frequency electric current to destroy tissues.

differentiation: *see* cell.

dysplasia: abnormal development of tissues or cells. Often used to describe changes suggestive, but not completely diagnostic, of malignancy.

endocrine glands: glands which make substances (hormones) fed directly into the blood stream having a profound effect upon growth, development, and many bodily functions. An example is the thyroid gland.

endometrium: the mucous membrane lining the womb.

endoscope: any instrument used for visual examination of an organ or area of the body not normally open to inspection. Often with a prefix to indicate the organ for which it is designed: thus laryngoscope, bronchoscope, gastroscope, cystoscope.

epithelium: a sheet of one or more layers of flattened cells attached to

Glossary

each other along their edges. Epithelium covers the outer surface of the body and lines the inner surface, such as the bowel.

gene: one of a series of units arranged on the chromosomes and responsible for the transmission of all the body's characteristics.

gland: a collection of cells which produce a secretion or excretion. Examples are the salivary glands which secrete the saliva and the sweat glands which excrete the sweat. The lymphatic glands are not true glands. They are a collection of lymphocytes enclosed within a fibrous capsule. The familiar word 'gland' is retained in this book, but they are better called lymph nodes.

glioma: a tumour of the brain or spinal cord arising from the neuroglia, the supporting tissue of the nervous system.

hormone: the secretion of an endocrine gland.

immunoglobulins: a class of protein substances present in the blood plasma; it includes the antibodies.

incidence: the frequency of the occurrence of a disease. Rate of incidence is usually expressed as the number of persons affected per 1 000 000 living per year. Age-adjusted incidence is the number of persons of a given age affected per year per 1 000 000 living persons of that age.

invasive: of cancer, when the growth has penetrated and infiltrated the surrounding normal tissues.

ionization: the production of charged atoms or molecules by radioactivity or X-ray.

isotopes: elements which are chemically identical, but differ in their atomic weights. A radioactive isotope is one which has an unstable nucleus emitting irradiation as it changes to a more stable form.

lymphangiography: lymphography. A method of demonstrating the lymphatic glands, especially those within the abdomen, by injecting contrast-medium into the lymphatic vessels in the foot and taking X-ray photographs when the contrast-medium has reached the level of the glands.

lymphoma: a cancer arising from cells of lymphatic tissue.

malignant: having the characteristics of cancer.

metastasis: the spread of cancer to parts remote from the primary growth, either through the lymphatic system or by the blood stream.

mongol: a common form of mental deficiency so-called on account of the supposed mongolian appearance of affected children.

morbidity: *see* incidence.

mortality: the number of persons dying. Mortality rate: the number of persons dying per year of a given disease per 1 000 000 living. Age-adjusted mortality (or death) rate: the number of persons of a given age dying per year of a given disease per 1 000 000 persons of that age living.

mesothorium: a radioactive isotope of radium.

Cancer – the facts

oncologist: a specialist in the treatment of cancer.

palliation: relief of symptoms without attempting cure.

pitchblende: a natural source of uranium occurring as a black mineral ore; the chief source of radium.

placebo: ineffective treatment prescribed to satisfy the patient's wish for therapeutic action.

protein: a member of a vast class of organic chemical compounds containing nitrogen and forming essential constituents of all living cells.

rad: the unit of the absorbed dose of radiation; used in radiotherapy.

radioactivity: a property of some elements which spontaneously emit alpha and beta particles and sometimes gamma rays as they change into another element.

radio-opaque: impervious or opaque to X-rays.

sarcoma: a cancer derived from connective tissue or from cells derived from it.

scanner: a device for recording the quantity of radioactivity emitted from tissues or other objects scanned.

screening: the examination of a population to determine the presence of disease.

secondary deposit: *see* metastasis.

staging: the allocation of a patient with cancer to one of a series of defined stages based on the extent of the primary tumour and the presence or absence of lymphatic or distant metastases.

subarachnoid space: the space between the pia mater and the arachnoid mater, the membranes which invest the brain and spinal cord, through which the cerebrospinal fluid circulates.

supervoltage therapy: radiotherapy employing a power in excess of 1 000 000 volts.

syndrome: a group of symptoms and signs occurring in association sufficiently frequently to form a characteristic disease picture.

teratoma: a group of tumours, some benign some malignant, derived from different primitive tissues of the embryo.

thermography: a method of recording photographically the temperature of the skin. Used in the diagnosis of cancer of the breast where the skin temperature overlying a tumour is usually raised.

undifferentiated: of cancer cells: cells which have the appearance of more primitive elements before the process of differentiation started. Usually indicative of an aggressive type of cancer.

uranium: a radioactive element occurring in pitchblende and other ores. It exists in three isotopes of which one – uranium-235 – was the basis of the atomic bomb.

virus: minute organisms invisible with the ordinary light microscope and passing through the finest filters. They live as parasites within cells and are responsible for many familiar infections such as the common cold, poliomyelitis, and influenza.

Index

Index